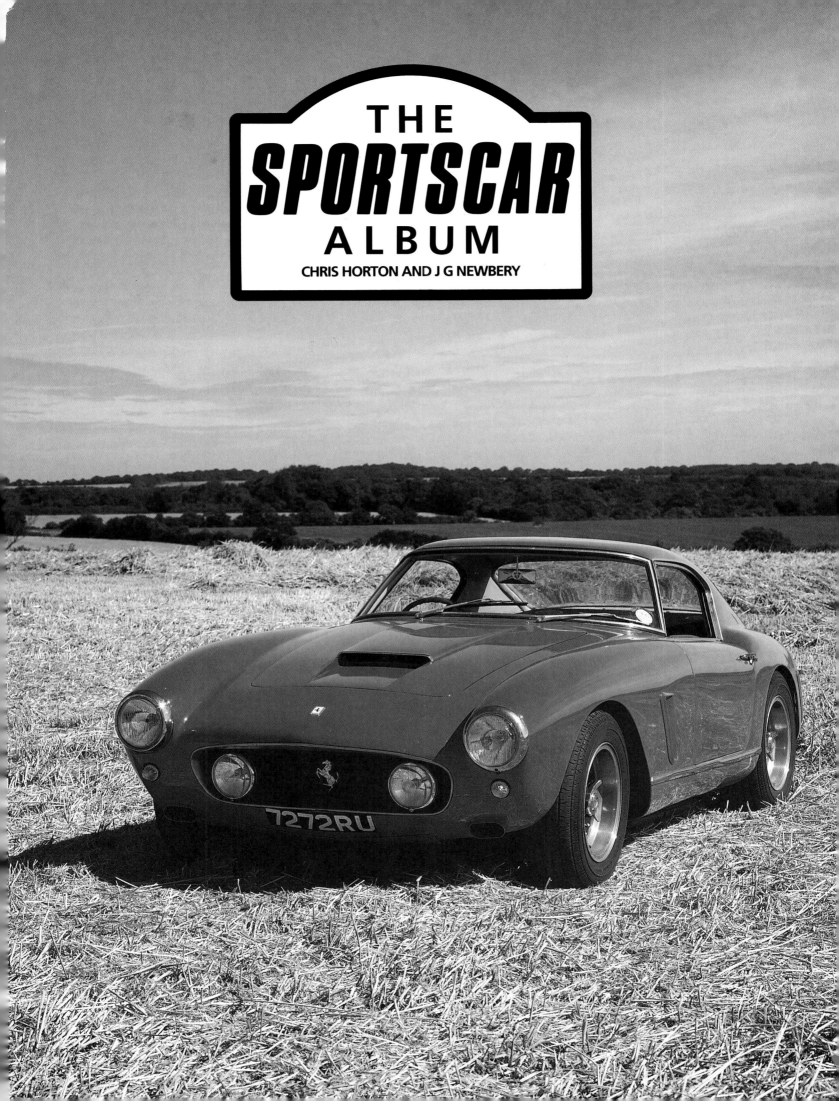

THE SPORTSCAR ALBUM

CHRIS HORTON AND J G NEWBERY

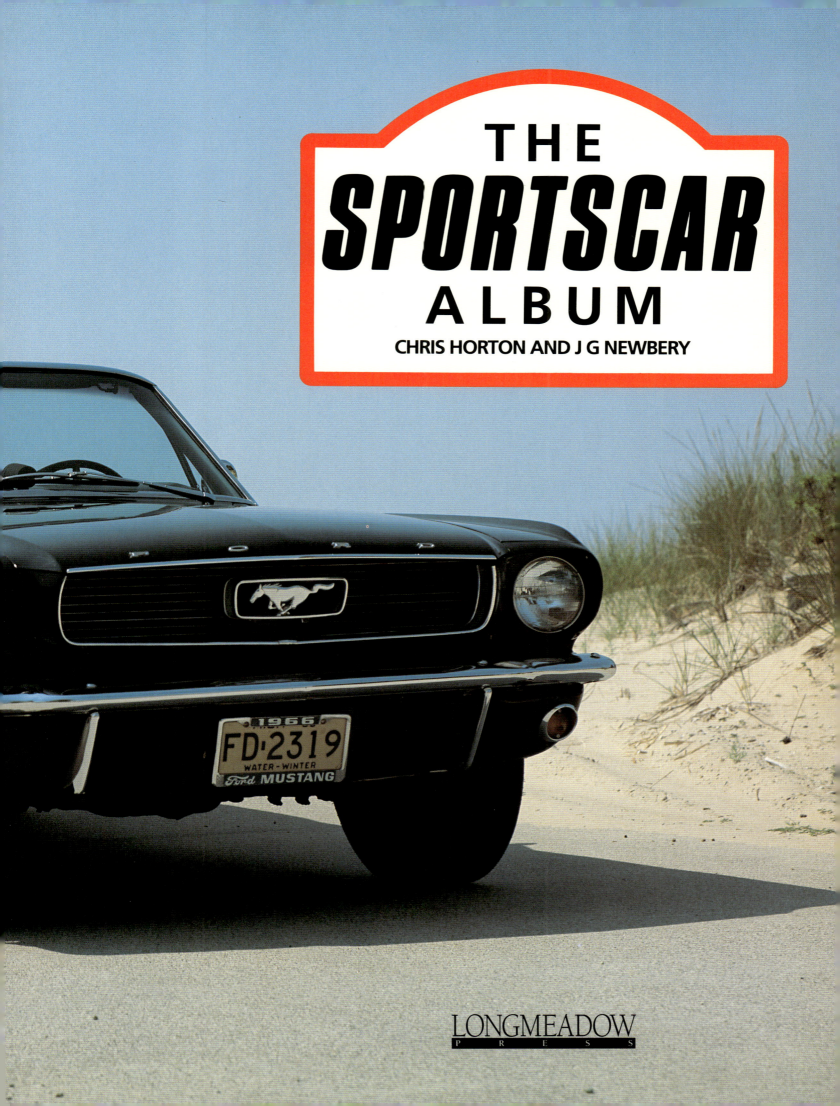

Copyright © 1993 Brompton Books Corporation

All rights reserved. No part of this book may be reproduced or utilized in any form or by any means, electronic or mechanical, including photocopying, recording or by any information storage and retrieval system, without permission in writing from the copyright holder.

This 1993 edition published by Longmeadow Press
201 High Ridge Road, Stamford CT 06904

Produced by Brompton Books Corporation
15 Sherwood Place, Greenwich CT 06830

ISBN 0-681-41868-0

Printed in Hong Kong

0 9 8 7 6 5 4 3 2 1

PAGE 1: The classic 1960 short-wheelbase Ferrari 250.

PAGES 2-3: A 1966 289cu.in. Mustang convertible.

THESE PAGES: A 1.1-liter Amilcar C6 in racing trim.

The authors wrote the following chapters:
Chris Horton: chapters 1-3
J G Newbery: chapters 4-7

Contents

Chapter 1: The Origins of the Sportscar	6
Chapter 2: The Roaring Twenties	36
Chapter 3: The Stylish Thirties	78
Chapter 4: From Austerity to Luxury	132
Chapter 5: The Swinging Sixties	168
Chapter 6: From Musclecar to Crisis	202
Chapter 7: The Challenge from the East	228
Index and Acknowledgments	255

Chapter ONE

The Origins of the Sportscar

It has long been customary to begin books like this by attempting to define and categorize their subject matter. In practice that has always been an impossible task, however, if only because no single criterion can possibly be applied to every one of what are now commonly considered sportscars. The simplest approach, if not necessarily the most helpful, is to suggest that anyone actively looking for a sportscar – and who has read this book – will invariably recognize one when they see it.

The origins of this apparently paradoxical statement can be traced back to the development of the first true motor cars in the mid-1880s. From then until the turn of the century there was plainly no such thing as a sportscar, yet such was the hazardous, pioneering nature of motoring at that time that it is equally accurate to say that each and every motor car of the period had the potential to be a sportscar.

One had to be wealthy or eccentric – and preferably both – to own a motor car before about 1900 and, difficult though it may be to imagine today, the vast majority of people drove purely for recreation – and not, as we now do, largely to get from A to B with a minimum of physical effort.

There were essentially two types of motor car by the beginning of the twentieth century: large and ponderous four-seaters with two- or sometimes four-cylinder front-mounted engines; and compact, light and lively runabouts (often with three wheels rather than four) powered by small and relatively high-speed engines (usually by de Dion) mounted at the rear.

Both strongly influenced the design of subsequent high-performance cars, but it was the former which led directly to the building of the first vehicles genuinely capable of 50mph – then as significant a psychological barrier as 100mph was during the 1950s or as 150mph remains today.

The reason for this was remarkably simple. The science of metallurgy was in its infancy, and not enough was known about the materials from which engines were manufactured to make them stay together at speeds much higher than about 800rpm. This necessarily limited their power output and the top speed of the cars to which they were fitted, but it quickly began to be appreciated by the more far-sighted designers that the key to better performance lay in a combination of engine size and number of cylinders. There was, in other words, no substitute for cubic inches.

The demand for more power and those cubic inches was further stimulated by the great motor-sporting events of the period. Road-racing was as popular in Europe in the early 1900s as Formula One is today, and winning a prestigious event could bring a manufact-

The Origins of the Sportscar 9

The Italian Isotta-Fraschinis (PREVIOUS PAGE) were similar to contemporary Mercedes. Here Trucco awaits the start of the 1908 Targa Florio. The Itala Grand Prix racing car (MAIN PICTURE) had a four-cylinder, 12-liter engine, developing 120bhp. With a four-cylinder engine of 5.9 liters, the successful 1901 Mercedes racing car (BELOW) developed 35bhp and was capable of nearly 50mph. This 1903 picture of the Napier 30hp racing car (RIGHT) shows Charles Jarrott at the wheel.

urer considerable fame and fortune. Wealthy amateurs would pay handsomely for replicas of the winning car (which often went into the following year's catalogue), and so a tradition became established, which continued until the mid-1920s, whereby the most popular racing cars were made available as road-going cars. Occasionally, but not always, they were detuned beforehand.

The first genuinely high-performance cars came from Germany, where the predominance of a wealthy leisured class hardly encouraged the building of cheap runabouts for the masses as it did in France and England and, to a lesser extent, America.

At Brooklands in 1907 S F Edge covered 1581 miles in 24 hours at the wheel of a 75bhp Napier 60 with a slightly modified engine. This car (LEFT) was built and sold as a road-going replica. The 1905 De Dietrich (RIGHT) exemplifies the high-powered two-seat runabout which was increasingly popular at the time. The four-cylinder 12-liter engine developed 70bhp and propelled the car at up to 70mph. The tiny 1908 Sizaire-Naudin (BELOW RIGHT) had a 1.5-liter engine in a rather crude chassis with sliding-pillar front suspension, but it was light, attractive and sold well.

The four-cylinder 28hp Canstatt-Daimler racing car of 1899 was claimed to be capable of 50mph – although it would have been a brave and experienced driver who achieved that – and a redesign by Paul Daimler in 1900 produced the famous 1901 Mercedes which, for the time, was a remarkably refined machine. Its 5.9-liter engine developed 35bhp at 1000rpm, and it set standards of chassis design which were to be emulated by other manufacturers for at least the next 30 years.

Few English manufacturers of the early 1900s appreciated the coming significance of high-performance cars for road use, however, concentrating instead on elegant town carriages and small, cheap and essentially very crude single-cylinder runabouts. From 1904 Daimler of Coventry took an active interest in competition, though, and its large four-cylinder models with chain drive were modestly successful in hillclimbs and trials – thanks mostly to their reliability rather than any outstanding dynamic abilities. Napier had joined the fray in 1903 by pioneering a six-cylinder side-valve engine, and it was in a modified Napier 60 that S F Edge covered 1581 miles in 24 hours at Brooklands in 1907.

In France de Dietrich became a fashionable marque. Charles Jarrott took third place in the 1903 Paris-Madrid road-race in a 45hp model, and the 12-liter 60, introduced in 1905, was capable of more than 70mph. The Belgian-built Métallurgique, introduced in 1907 and extremely advanced for its day, was even faster. Its 10-liter engine developed 100bhp at 1400rpm, it featured shaft drive instead of the more normal chains of the period and, with a four-speed gearbox, could easily top 80mph.

Perhaps more significant than this still-impressive performance, however, was the two-seat bodywork which by now was an increasingly common feature of cars with sporting pretensions. In practice, sportscar bodies were usually little more than productionized, road-going versions of the minimal coachwork required by contemporary Grand Prix formulae and, like the chassis of that 1901 Mercedes, they set a standard for what we now know as vintage sportscars which lasted until 1939 – and later than that in some cases.

Italy was a relative latecomer to car production, but by 1908 the successes achieved by Fiat in international events had created considerable interest in its products. A large Itala with a four-cylinder, 7.4-liter engine developing 40bhp won the famous Peking-to-Paris event of 1907 (this was more an endurance event like the modern Paris-Dakar than a conventional road-race), and earlier still, in 1906, Isotta-Fraschini had become one of the first users of overhead camshafts with their 120bhp racing car.

Of rather more interest here, though, is the team of 1200cc Isottas which took part in the 1908 Coupe des Voiturettes. They were sound and attractive little cars designed by Ettore Bugatti, but they never achieved the popularity of contemporaries like the crude but surprisingly fast single-cylinder Sizaire-Naudin, and it was only during the 1920s that the aptly named voiturette was to emerge as a definitive sportscar class in its own right.

What really promoted the cause and development of the sports car in Europe, however, was first the Herkomer Trophy (run in 1905, 1906 and 1907) and then the so-called Prince Henry Tours of 1908 to 1911 inclusive. The first of the Prince Henry Tours, in 1908, was remarkable in the way the rules had clearly been stretched to their very limits by some of the more enterprising entrants: many of the competing cars had flamboyantly flared fenders and tiny running-boards, and in some cases outrageous horizontal fenders running the length of the flush-sided, boat-decked bodywork. There

The Origins of the Sportscar 11

were, inevitably, protests about what were considered by some to be racing cars in touring trim, but again this was one of the first manifestations of the classic sportscar look which was to last until the late 1930s.

Even more significant was one of the cars which was developed specifically for the penultimate Prince Henry Tour in 1910. Designed by Ferdinand Porsche (later responsible for the Volkswagen Beetle, as well as a range of sportscars bearing his own name) the 27/80 Austro-Daimler had a 5.7-liter single-overhead-camshaft, four-cylinder engine developing some 95bhp; a distinctively flared body (which, interestingly, featured four seats rather than the two one might have expected); and performance, steering, roadholding and braking which remained ahead of its contemporaries for many years.

The Prince Henry Austro-Daimler was, in short, the first sportscar actually designed as such and intended for volume production. It was spectacularly successful in the event from which it derived its name; it achieved instant recognition for its manufacturer; it established a fashion for large, long-stroke engines which flourished in Europe until the early 1930s; and it remained on sale until as late as 1914 (although its original chain drive was superseded by a shaft in 1912).

No less significant was the 1910 Prince Henry Vauxhall. Like the Austro-Daimler, this was developed specifically for that year's event of the same name (in this case from the car which had taken part in the Royal Automobile Club's 2000-mile trial of 1908). It featured a 3-liter engine producing 60bhp which, thanks to careful attention to lubrication and piston design, could run at the then virtually unheard of speed of 2800rpm. The Vauxhall's vaguely torpedo-style bodywork was flush-sided with no noticeable junction between the hood and scuttle, and the radiator was markedly pointed in the fashion of the day. In practice the Vauxhalls were outgunned by the best of the European opposition, but the car went into volume production in 1911 (alongside the standard 20hp tourer) and, with a guaranteed top speed of 65mph, it has the distinction of being the first true sportscar to be built in England.

Several other factors influenced the development of the European sportscar before World War I. In Britain one of the most significant was the opening of the famous banked circuit at Brooklands in 1907. Before this, any sportscar manufacturer – or even sportscar owner – had to go abroad to travel consistently quickly without falling foul of the 20mph speed limit, and as a result the track was for many years one of the world's top automotive record-breaking centers.

Such was the layout of the circuit, however, with its steep, high-speed banking and long straights, that engine design soon came to have rather more bearing on performance than chassis design. The first cars to appear at Brooklands were stripped-down touring chassis, or else the ex-Grand Prix cars so fashionable among the more affluent motorists of the time; but between 1910 and 1914 there was a shift towards smaller-engined cars from British manufacturers such as Cross-

ley, Vauxhall, Straker-Squire and Sunbeam, and all were designed specifically for sporting events. Almost all had four-cylinder side-valve engines of between two and four liters, and they often defeated much more powerful cars from the Continent thanks to their reliability and simplicity.

In France the light-car races held from 1906 to 1910 had done much to advance the development of small, fast machines with high-efficiency four-cylinder engines. Winning models were often put straight into limited production with touring bodywork, and by 1911 this resulted in road-going gems like the 3-liter Delage – complete with a five-speed overdrive gearbox – and the 1460cc, overhead-camshaft Bugatti – which was, in fact, one of the first cars to bear the famous designer's name.

Some French manufacturers persisted with older single-cylinder designs, however, and among the most well-known of these (if not the most refined) was the 1.5-liter Sizaire-Naudin. It featured a crude sliding-pillar front suspension system and a strange "gearbox" consisting of a number of concentric propeller shafts which, with practice, could be meshed with the single crown wheel. However, it was light, stylish, cheap and fairly lively, and, to what must have been the lasting irritation of manufacturers like Delage and Bugatti, it sold surprisingly well.

Old habits died hard in Germany, however. By 1912 Benz was selling what was effectively its 1911 Land Speed Record-breaker with a massive 22-liter engine (even in road trim this was capable of over 110mph; at Brooklands it had achieved a breathtaking 142mph), although the company did produce some rather more practical fast tourers: first the four-cylinder, 9.5-liter 90 of 1912, and then the six-cylinder, overhead-camshaft, 7.2-liter 28/95 of 1914.

Large cars were not particularly popular in Britain at this time, yet from 1911 to 1914 no less a manufacturer than Rolls-Royce offered its Silver Ghost chassis with light, touring bodywork to produce a sporting car in the truest sense of the phrase. It was one of the largest and most elegant cars ever built. With only 50bhp from its 7.4-liter engine it wasn't unduly fast, but it set standards of refinement which in many respects would have been hard to beat even half a century later. A Silver Ghost won the Spanish Grand Prix in 1913, and in the same year a team of works cars dominated the Alpine Trials in Austria.

One of the most technically interesting prewar sportscars came from Italy. The 100hp Isotta-Fraschini dated from 1910, but it became available in short-chassis form in 1913 and is reckoned even now to be one of the best-looking sporting cars of the period. Its 10.6-liter engine featured a single overhead camshaft operating four valves per cylinder, and the performance provided by its 125bhp was made all the more usable by genuine four-wheel braking. Most other manufacturers had dropped this idea in 1911, arguing that front-wheel brakes were a dangerous and unnecessary complexity

The Origins of the Sportscar 13

The 15hp Crossley – this is a 1912/13 model – had a conventional side-valve four-cylinder engine (RIGHT), but its relatively high performance encouraged the company to build a competition variant called the Shelsley. The Stutz Bearcat (BELOW) remains one of the most famous American sportscars. This 1914 model would have had a four-cylinder engine of 5.4-liters and a three-speed transmission; note the chain drive.

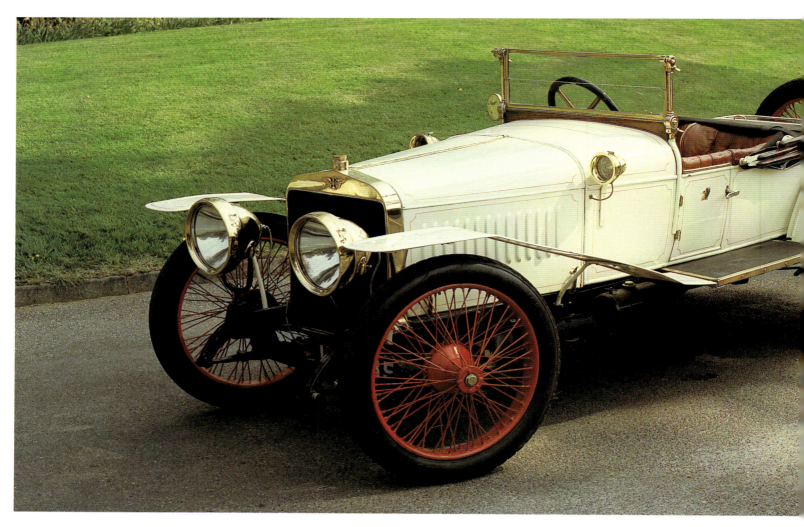

The Origins of the Sportscar 15

The Hispano-Suiza Alfonso, named after King Alfonso XIII of Spain, was one of the prettiest sportscars of the period. Its four-cylinder 3.6-liter engine produced 64bhp at 2300rpm and in two-seat form – like this 1912 example (LEFT) – it was capable of around 70mph. The Stutz Bearcat's closest rival was the Mercer Raceabout (BELOW LEFT). Like the Stutz it had hardly any bodywork to speak of, and its 5-liter Continental-built engine enabled it to attain a guaranteed 70mph. By 1914 the original Prince Henry Vauxhall (named after the motor-sporting event devised by Prince Henry of Prussia) had evolved into this 4.5-liter 30/98 model (BELOW).

(as, indeed, they were, given that little was known about combining steered wheels with brakes that worked when they were supposed to, and only when they were supposed to).

Spain, too, produced some fascinating sportscars with highly creditable performance. Designed by the Swiss Marc Birkigt and built in Barcelona, the four-cylinder Alfonso XIII Hispano-Suiza (named after the country's reigning monarch, an enthusiastic motorist who drove himself whenever possible) had a simple 3.6-liter engine producing 64bhp at 2300rpm, and a modest three-speed gearbox. It was imported to Britain from 1911 and, with good looks and a guaranteed top speed of 72mph in the short-chassis version, it sold well.

There was a gradual reduction in sportscar dimensions during this period, but one of the most extreme and intriguing manifestations of this downsizing was the cyclecar which, despite modest performance and often rather crude design and construction, was incredibly popular in France and Britain from about 1910. The cyclecar, by definition, weighed less than 6cwt (305kg), had an engine capacity of less than 1100cc, and often owed more to motorcycle practice than the car world proper.

Two of the best-known cyclecars were the French Bédélia and the British GN. The former, developed by Borbeau and Devaux, had a front-mounted, air-cooled twin-cylinder engine driving the rear axle via an enormously long belt (the racing model's wheelbase was well over two meters); a swivelling front axle controlled by a crude wire-and-bobbin arrangement; and, perhaps strangest of all, a tandem seating arrangement in which the driver sat behind his passenger (who was also expected to change gear). It was a crude and even dangerous device, but it did surprisingly well in competition.

16 The Sportscar Album

Of rather more conventional appearance – and widely considered to be one of the best of the economy cyclecars – was the GN developed in Britain from 1910 by H R Godfrey and Archie Frazer-Nash. It featured an air-cooled V-twin engine, a light ash frame, and belt drive. By 1913 a heavier Grand Prix version, designed for the voiturette races at Amiens in northern France, was capable of 55mph. Frazer-Nash later went on to build his own car of the same name, and with its unique chain-and-dog-clutch transmission this was to become one of the most famous sportscars built between the two world wars.

So far we've looked purely at European sportscars, but on the other side of the Atlantic the American sportscar was evolving throughout this period as a definite type in its own right. This occurred mostly as a result of the prevailing geographic and demographic conditions and, with one or two notable exceptions, there was very little influence from Europe.

The most remarkable feature of early American cars – tourers and sportscars alike – was their mechanical sophistication. The latter may have had primitive chassis, often carrying little more than two seats, a large fuel tank and minimal weather protection, but at the same time they nearly always had soft, long-travel suspension to cope with the appalling (but mostly straight) roads, powerful and reliable multi-cylinder engines, electric starters, synchromesh transmissions and (even though the result was in many cases still less effective than their European counterparts) hydraulic braking systems. Significantly, the prewar American sportscar also enjoyed the benefit of an extra three years of production over its European rivals – America didn't enter the war until 1917 – so even postwar models were commensurately more developed than those from European manufacturers.

Although it was an evolutionary blind alley, one of the first high-performance American cars was powered not by a petrol-driven internal-combustion engine but by a steam engine. (Steamers were very popular in America at this time and were built in large numbers until the mid-1920s.) The Stanley brothers of Massachusetts built their first steam car in 1906 and soon afterwards took the Land Speed Record at a staggering 127mph with an engine of less than 3.5 liters. Even the brothers' wonderfully named Gentleman's Speedy Roadster, first offered in the same year, was capable of more than 75mph.

This period also saw the introduction of high-performance American cars of more conventional layout. Highly regarded at the time, but largely forgotten since, was Smith and Mabley of New York who began production in 1904, and by 1907 had developed a 50bhp four-cylinder car of 9.7-liters. Soon afterwards the company suffered financial problems, but it was relaunched in 1908 and its cars, renamed Simplex, enjoyed a highly successful competition career until America entered the war in 1917. It was, perhaps, a result of the company having previously imported various European cars –

not least Mercedes – that its products initially bore a more than passing resemblance to contemporary Mercedes.

Sportscar racing was extremely popular in the US just before World War I, and it was mostly as a result of this that Stutz cars achieved lasting fame. Harry C Stutz built his first car in 1911 to prove the axles and transmission he was supplying to other manufacturers, and although it only finished 11th in that year's event at Indianapolis, a road-going version entered production in 1912. The even more famous Bearcat appeared in 1914 with a 5.4-liter four-cylinder engine and a three-speed gearbox built in unit with the rear axle. This wasn't an entirely successful arrangement, but with little more to pull than the weight of its chassis the Bearcat remains one of the most exciting prewar US sportscars, and is highly sought-after to this day.

But by far the most important prewar American sportscar was the Mercer Raceabout. The Mercer Company, of Mercer County in New Jersey, began building medium-sized four-cylinder cars in 1909, and in 1911 chief designer Finlay Robertson Porter introduced the Type 35 cars which remained in production until 1915. These featured a four-cylinder side-valve engine of 4.9 liters (when many other manufacturers were still building 12-liter cars), dual ignition, a multi-plate clutch and shaft drive. The maximum power was 60bhp and maximum engine speed was a creditable 2500rpm. Even so, the cars were capable of 75mph and could cruise comfortably at 60mph.

What really distinguished the Raceabout, however, was its styling, making it one of the earliest cars to sell as much on its looks as it did on performance. With long, flowing fenders, short running-boards and a bolster-type fuel tank in the tail the Raceabout was like nothing else on the road. The only weather equipment was a vestigial (and largely useless) monocle-type windscreen bolted to the steering column – which, like many of the Raceabout's contemporaries, was placed on the right-hand side of the car.

The Raceabout had an illustrious competition history (despite a somewhat fragile chassis and marginal brakes) and approximately two road-going cars were built each week from 1911 to 1915. Very few examples of America's best-known sportscar survive, however, and it was the big between-the-wars sedans and flamboyant roadsters like the Auburn and Cord which really captured the imagination of latter-day enthusiasts.

Just as racing is said to improve the breed so, in the case of the road-going sportscar, did the apparently improbable stimulus of World War I. The sudden demand for light, powerful and reliable aircraft engines inevitably continued the development of engine design where racing had abandoned it in 1914, and the widespread use of aluminum pistons, pressurized lubrication systems, lighter valvegear and much tougher bearing materials significantly raised crankshaft speeds and specific power outputs. These advances would lead to a new era for the sportscar when the war finally ended.

Rolls-Royce was a noted manufacturer of sporting cars before World War I. The so-called Alpine Eagle cars (ABOVE) were developed from the team cars which took part in the 1913 Austrian Alpine trials, and featured four-speed gearboxes, aluminum pistons, larger-capacity radiators and better brakes than their predecessors. At the other end of the scale was the diminutive GN (RIGHT), which by the time of this 1914 model had become one of the best of the economy British cyclecars. Despite its tiny twin-cylinder engine the Grand Prix model was capable of over 50mph.

18 The Sportscar Album

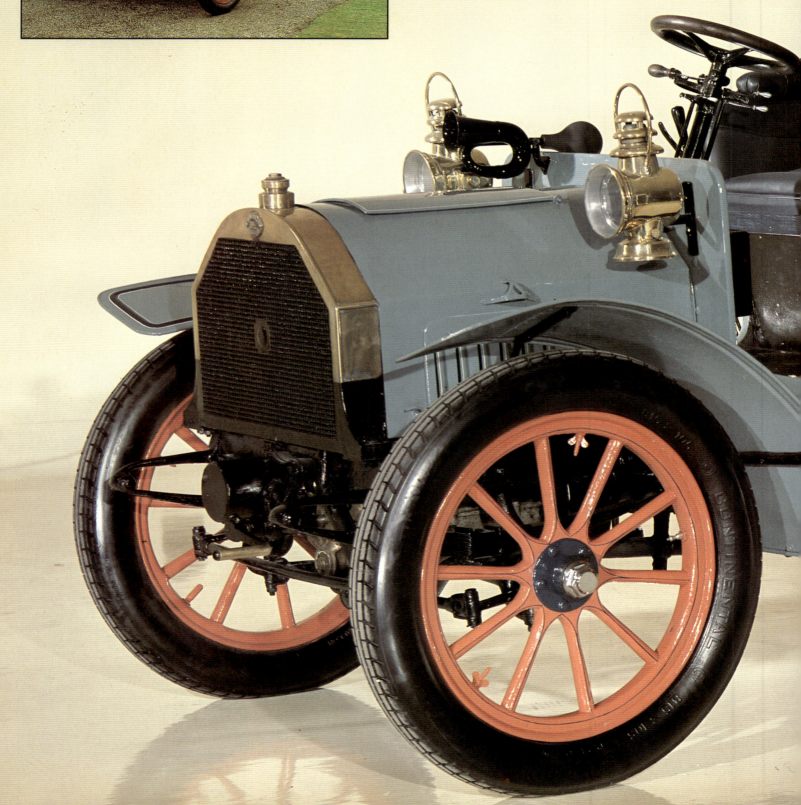

The Origins of the Sportscar 19

Germany at the turn of the century saw the development of a number of technically advanced machines such as this 1902 Opel (MAIN PICTURE), and enthusiastic owners soon organized their own local sporting events. The 1903 60hp two-seat Mercedes (FAR LEFT) was derived from the competitors in that year's Gordon Bennett Cup. It had a 9-liter engine and final drive by chain; it is considered one of the most important early sportscars. The Renault in which Marcel Renault finished second in the 1902 Paris-to-Vienna road race featured a 3.8-liter four-cylinder engine (LEFT).

Mercedes racing cars achieved considerable success in the early years of the century. The 120hp cars of 1905/6 (LEFT AND ABOVE LEFT) had four cylinder engines of no less than 16 liters. Note the almost non-existent bodywork and, in the case of the lower car, the lack of front mudguards. Brasier was a very conservative French manufacturer, but wins in the 1904 and 1905 Gordon Bennett Trophy brought it considerable fame throughout the world. This racing version (ABOVE) again has vestigial coachwork, but there was also a four-seater 16hp tourer. Charles Jarrott took third place in the Paris-Madrid road-race in a 45hp De Dietrich similar to this 24hp model (RIGHT).

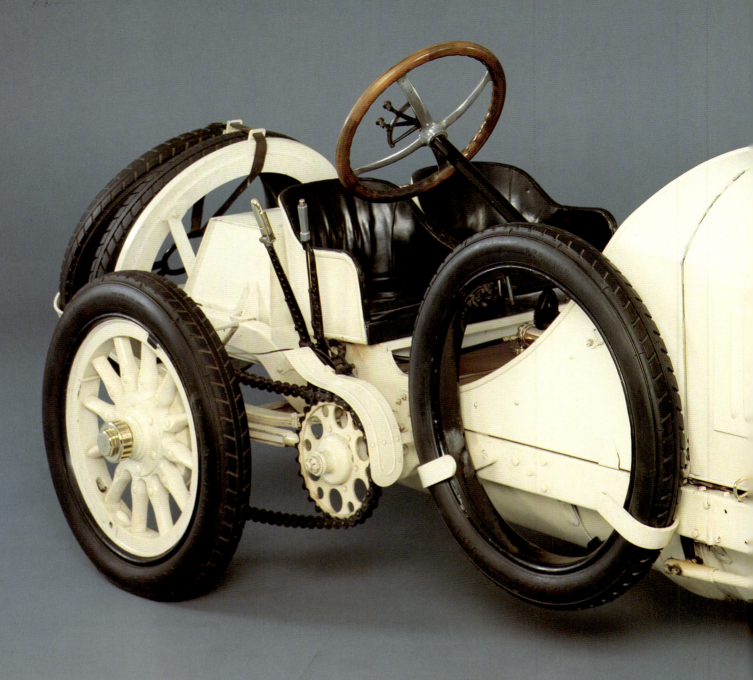

The Grand Prix Benz of 1908 (MAIN PICTURE) had a four-cylinder engine, chain drive and the scanty racing bodywork so typical of the period. Italian manufacturer S.C.A.T. produced a range of modest-specification cars from 1906, all with four-speed gearboxes and shaft drive. This 1908 racing car (LEFT) is seen at the so-called Four Inch Race.

Itala produced a number of sporting tourers in addition to its better-known Grand Prix cars. This 1908 model (LEFT) was photographed at the Prescott hillclimb course in 1975. Steam-powered cars have achieved sporting status: this 20hp 1908 Stanley (BELOW, FAR LEFT) was easily capable of 75mph. The 1908 six-cylinder 5-liter R-Type (BELOW LEFT) was one of the few truly sporting cars from the British firm of Napier. Cagno's Itala (RIGHT) stands on the weighbridge in Bologna before the start of the 1908 Coppa Florio, an event for Grand Prix-type cars. Sporting models from Calthorpe featured two- or four-seat polished aluminum bodies and alloy reciprocating engine parts which were drilled for lightness. This 1908 model (BELOW) was photographed at the Four Inch Race.

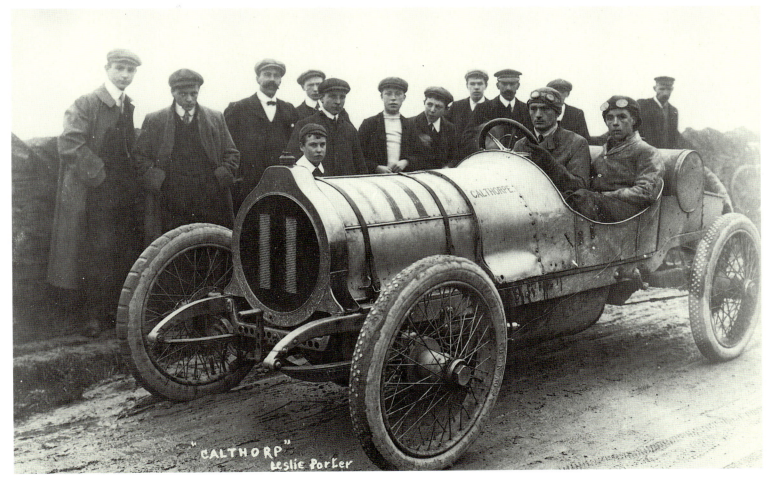

The Origins of the Sportscar 27

Rolls-Royce chassis formed the basis of some of the most beautiful sporting cars before World War I. This 1914 Silver Ghost (ABOVE LEFT) has a body by Schebera-Schapiro of Berlin. The 1909 8hp De Dion-Bouton (LEFT) featured a 1.8-liter four-cylinder engine with pair-cast cylinders. The four-cylinder Mercedes 90 of 1911/12 (ABOVE) was the first to bear the pointed radiator, and often had disk wheels, as here. The 9.5-liter engine had two exhaust valves and one inlet valve per cylinder. The 1910 Rolls-Royce Silver Ghost (RIGHT) was a sporting car more by accident than design, combining high performance with astonishing refinement. Its six-cylinder 7.4-liter engine only developed around 50bhp but in 1911 a Silver Ghost drove all the way from London to Edinburgh in top gear at an average of 24mph.

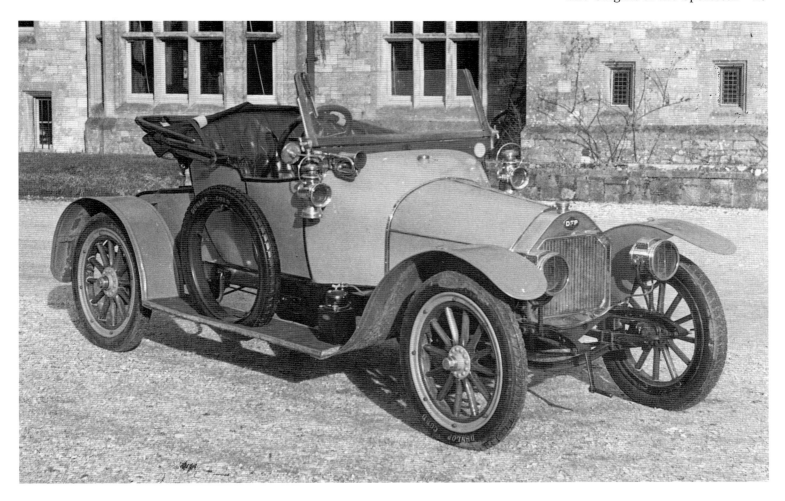

The 8hp Morgan three-wheeler of 1913 (ABOVE, FAR LEFT) was powered by a side-valve JAP engine of 1.1 liters. It was safer than most contemporary three-wheelers thanks to its above-average roadholding. De Dietrich enjoyed a good reputation in road-racing in the early years of the century but then settled down to building robust touring cars under the name Lorraine-Dietrich. The company's last serious competition appearance was at the 1908 French Grand Prix but for 1912 it built this 15-liter monster (LEFT). The 10/12hp DFP introduced in 1910 featured a four-cylinder 1.6-liter engine with magneto ignition, thermo-syphon cooling, cone clutch and three-speed gearbox. This car (ABOVE) is a 1913 Series M two-seater.

30 The Sportscar Album

The Crouch (LEFT) began life as a three-wheeled cyclecar, but was offered as a four-wheeler from 1913. The distinctive short nose concealed a 1-liter water-cooled twin-cylinder engine by Coventry-Simplex. This 3-liter 20hp Napier tourer (BELOW) dates from about 1915. The DI Delage (RIGHT) is from 1913. One of the last Mercedes cars to be built before World War I was this 117hp racing car (BELOW RIGHT).

This 1912 Simplex (ABOVE) was one of the last American cars to be fitted with chain drive. Note also the right-hand driving position and the almost non-existent rear bodywork. German cars of the immediate postwar period, like this Benz sports tourer (LEFT), were essentially revised prewar designs. Front-wheel brakes appeared from about 1923. This 1903 40hp Winton Bullet (ABOVE RIGHT) was one of the two cars with which the American company entered that year's Gordon Bennett Trophy. Both retired during the race, but a similar 80hp car later set various records. The 4-liter Straker-Squire achieved some fame in the postwar period. This 1918 model (RIGHT) had a six-cylinder engine with separate cylinders and exposed valvegear.

The Biddle was a popular American sporting roadster. This 1918 Model K (LEFT) had a 7-liter Duesenberg engine, and is seen here at the first Anglo-American Vintage Car Rally at Silverstone in 1954. The most famous Stutz of all, the Bearcat, was in production from 1914 to 1924 – this car (BELOW) is a 1918 model. William and George Kissel built their first car in 1905, but the 1918 car (RIGHT) was the first overtly sporting Kissel. This particular car has been substantially customized. This 1919 Stutz Bearcat (BELOW RIGHT) has British registration plates.

The Roaring Twenties

The sportscars that emerged after World War I began to show substantial reductions in engine size and a far greater reliance on the gearbox to provide reasonable – and in some cases very rapid – acceleration. Prior to 1914 the gearbox was seen primarily as a device to start the large-engined cars of the period from rest, or to allow them to climb the steepest hills, but in postwar machines like the new 3-liter Bentley the gearbox provided not only useful and usable performance in each ratio, but also a considerable overlap between them.

Chassis design, however, still wasn't progressing at quite such a satisfying rate. There was a move toward the rigid mounting of the engine and gearbox in place of the detachable subframe which had been popular before the war, and this significantly improved handling thanks to the better bracing it provided, but the introduction of front-wheel brakes between about 1920 in Europe and 1923 in Britain wasn't the unmitigated blessing it might have seemed. They certainly provided much more consistent stopping power in a straight line, but there was no guarantee that they wouldn't be activated by the simple act of turning the steering wheel; and, by adding considerably to the front axle's unsprung weight, they also had very detrimental effects on steering and handling which were never satisfactorily dealt with until the development of effective independent front suspension in the early 1930s.

Pre-eminent among English sportscar manufacturers of the early postwar period was Vauxhall, even though in more recent years, and as part of the vast US-based General Motors empire, it has concentrated almost exclusively on family sedans. Its four-cylinder 30/98 was actually introduced before the war, but very few had been built and it was only after its re-introduction in 1919 that the so-called E-type became available in significant numbers.

Thanks to its elegant four-seater coachwork and brisk performance – 100mph was possible with the optional racing bodywork, although the 30/98 never competed to anything like the same extent as the contemporary 3-liter Bentley – it was one of the most desirable touring cars on the market until its increasing obsolescence in the mid-1920s. Indeed, Vauxhall itself unwittingly provided a virtually irrefutable definition of the sportscar (which, generally speaking, still holds good today) in its catalogue description of the 30/98 as "a very refined fast touring car capable of high average speeds and suitable for competition work."

If the Vauxhall, like many of its contemporaries, was essentially a prewar design, then the 3-liter Bentley was new from end to end. It was also one of the first British sportscars to be announced after the war – in May 1919 to be precise, although the first production cars weren't actually delivered until 1921. It sold fairly

The Invicta (PREVIOUS PAGE) was a popular British make. This one is a 3-liter from 1927. The pioneering front-wheel-drive Alvis of the early 1920s (LEFT) was technically highly creditable, but it was noisy and difficult to drive. It had a 1.5-liter engine with overhead valves, a four-speed gearbox and the option of a Roots supercharger. Postwar Bentleys were relatively crude cars, but they were strong, powerful and reliable. This car (ABOVE RIGHT) is a 1926 3-liter long-chassis Speed model with a body by Barker. In 1926 Mercedes and Benz had merged. The 38/250 SS (RIGHT) appeared in 1928 with a 7-liter supercharged engine developing 200bhp. The same chassis was used for a much less flamboyant tourer and also for the 130mph SSKL.

well thanks to its reliability, excellent handling and brisk performance (despite its relatively high price), and from 1922 a modest competition program boosted sales quite considerably, particularly after a 3-liter won at Le Mans in 1924.

One of the first postwar European sportscars was the 7.2-liter Hispano-Suiza, again launched in 1919. With a six-cylinder engine of 6597cc derived from one of Marc Birkigt's most successful military aircraft engines, fine handling and roadholding, and a top speed of about 75mph, it was immensely popular among the more affluent sporting French motorists of the time. There were several attempts by other manufacturers to copy its appearance, but it retained its following, and remained in production until as late as 1935.

German cars of the immediate postwar period were, perhaps not surprisingly, mostly revised prewar designs, and since their export was not exactly encouraged, they tended to be rare outside Germany itself. Mercedes updated its 7.2-liter 28/95 of 1914 and this was modestly successful in European hillclimbs and speed trials, although it was as the chassis on which the company carried out its supercharging experiments – and which in the late 1920s led to some of the most breathtaking sportscars of all time – that it achieved its greatest significance.

In France in the early 1920s there was a great deal of interest in long-distance races on road circuits for sporting four-seaters in more or less standard trim, and this prompted the development of some interesting and successful cars built specifically for such events. Lorraine-Dietrich, for example, was better-known for its robust tourers, but from 1924 to 1926 it entered a number of specially prepared 3.5-liter cars at Le Mans. All featured rather fragile twin-carburettor engines with overhead valves operated by exposed pushrods, together with three-speed gearboxes and powerful servo brakes; maximum speed was about 95mph.

The technical improvements brought about by World War I also led to an increasing interest in what were then considered very small engines. Before the war few cars built for serious use had engines of much below three liters, but by 1922 their performance could be equalled, if not bettered, by most 1.5-liter models. British manufacturers such as Alvis, MG and Riley were later to excel in this field, but it was Bugatti, with his T23 'Brescia' of 1920 (named after the Italian town where it achieved its first victory), who first demonstrated exactly what 1.5 liters could do. Indeed, with its 1496cc engine, multi-plate clutch and four-speed gearbox giving a maximum speed of about 85mph, the T23 was easily the fastest small car on the market for a time. Not surprisingly, it caused a sensation.

At least as advanced as Bugatti's designs, and certainly even less conventional, was the Italian Lancia Lambda which was launched in 1922. This seems, on the face of it, to have been far more a four-seat tourer than a true sportscar, but its then-unique unitary-construction chassis, powerful cable-operated brakes and low unsprung weight provided superb handling; while an extremely narrow-angle V4 engine of 2120cc developing 50bhp at 3000rpm meant the car was good for

The Type 35 Bugatti won innumerable sporting events between 1924 and 1930. It was fitted with engines as small as 1.1 liters, but this 1926 Type 35B (LEFT) had a 2.3-liter straight-eight. Touring versions were also available. The Lancia Lambda (RIGHT) was a revolutionary design when it was introduced in 1922. It had a very narrow-angle V4 engine, a combined chassis and body built on unitary-construction principles, and four-wheel brakes. The 2.1-liter engine developed 50bhp at 3000rpm, and even early cars were capable of 70mph.

at least 70mph. At the time, this was still way beyond the reach of most genuine tourers.

Light English sportscars were crude by comparison. Almost without exception they achieved their high performance (remarkably, from simple side-valve engines) by means of very light bodywork and high axle ratios, but their typical maximum speeds of around 60mph were more than enough to give them a comfortable lead over their larger touring contemporaries and to justify their definition as sportscars: most of these tourers were hard-pushed to better 45mph.

One of the first exponents of this genre was Percy Riley with his 70mph 11/40 Sports Model which, because of its striking bare-aluminum body and contrasting painted fenders, was popularly known as the Redwing. From 1922 Alvis offered a similar 12/40 Sports Model which was guaranteed to exceed 60mph, and the subsequent 12/50, with its characteristic "duck's back" bodywork, went on to become the best-selling 1.5-liter model of the period.

The second half of the 1920s saw further notable advances in car design and technology. Maximum speeds rose markedly with the long-overdue development of four-wheel brakes which actually worked, and by 1930, 60mph was as commonplace as it had been remarkable ten years earlier. Small six-cylinder engines became increasingly popular, and apart from one or two manufacturers – notably Bentley and Mercedes-Benz – the large-capacity engine was virtually extinct. At the other end of the scale the sporting cyclecar had all but disappeared, too.

Chassis design still lagged some way behind engine technology, though. There was a gradual lowering of centers of gravity to provide better cornering, while springs became flatter and stiffer, and moderately effective friction-type dampers to control the suspension movement eventually came into fairly widespread use; but unsprung weight was climbing inexorably and steering systems tended to become increasingly low-geared to reduce the not-inconsiderable effort required at the wheel.

Among those who remained faithful to the idea of large-capacity engines were Bentley in Britain and Mercedes-Benz in Germany. The original 3-liter Bentley was supplemented by a four-cylinder 4.5-liter model in 1927 (fitted with a Roots supercharger from about 1928); the six-cylinder Speed Six arrived in 1929; and, in 1930, the apotheosis of the large-engined British sportscar appeared in the form of the 8-liter Bentley. This produced no less than 220bhp from its six-cylinder engine and, with the right development and backing, could easily have been a serious competitor to the 38/250 Mercedes which was to dominate sportscar racing in Europe in the early 1930s.

The contemporary cars of Mercedes-Benz were, if anything, even more spectacular than the Bentleys. Ferdinand Porsche joined the company in 1926 and immediately began experimenting with supercharging as a means of boosting performance. The 33/180 Model K appeared in the same year with an overhead-camshaft six-cylinder engine of 6.2-liters and an ingenious system whereby flooring the throttle pedal engaged the

clutch of the supercharger's driving mechanism to force-feed the engine.

With a high chassis the 33/180 was, however, a rather dangerous machine, and in 1927 it was replaced by the 36/220 Model S which, in addition to a much lower center of gravity, also had far more effective brakes. The 36/220 took the first three places in the 1927 German Grand Prix and in 1928 was supplemented by the still-larger 38/250 SS. Even in standard form this could exceed 110mph and, as the sports-racing SSKL with 300bhp, it was capable of well over 130mph. At the time this was a truly breathtaking speed for a road car.

The nearest French equivalent to the Mercedes was the Bugatti Type 35. Launched in 1924 this had a single-overhead-camshaft straight-eight engine and a quite superbly engineered chassis, and such was its performance that it virtually dominated its class of sportscar racing from 1925 to as late as 1930. The 115bhp roller-bearing engine was safe to 5000rpm and propelled the car to a maximum speed of about 110mph.

In Italy by far the best of the medium-size high-performers came from Alfa Romeo: it was in an Alfa that Enzo Ferrari began his competition career in the 1920 Targa Florio road race. The first Alfa Romeo sportscar to enter production was the six-cylinder 22/90 of 2994cc. In short-chassis form this was guaranteed to top 85mph and such was its popularity that it remained virtually unchanged until 1928. In 1927 the 22/90 was supplemented by a 1500cc tourer with a six-cylinder engine, interesting not least for its later acquisition of two gear-driven overhead camshafts and a Roots supercharger. With open sports bodywork this car weighed considerably less than a metric ton and enjoyed an active sports-racing career from 1928.

By far the most famous Alfa of this period, however, was the 1750 which appeared in 1929. With a larger version of the 1500's six-cylinder engine, and available either with single or twin overhead camshafts, it was a fast and superbly controllable machine which could reach 100mph with ease. Its success in events like the Targa Florio and Mille Miglia have long made it one of the most sought-after sportscars of its period, if not one of the most sought-after sportscars ever built. Today it is virtually priceless.

In America during the 1920s the large-capacity engine still reigned supreme, although this tended to produce sportscars by default rather than by design. Duesenberg, strongly influenced by Bugatti's designs, launched its 4.2-liter Model A tourer in 1921, but despite good performance and a fairly advanced mechanical specification – including a straight-eight engine with a single overhead camshaft and hydraulically operated four-wheel brakes – it was a rather ordinary-looking car and less than 100 were built by the time it ceased production in 1926.

Duesenberg the company was taken over by Cord at around this time, however, and Duesenberg the man became heavily involved in the 6.8-liter straight-eight Cord Model J which appeared in 1928. With four valves per cylinder, a five-bearing crankshaft, and a special

The Alfa Romeo RL (ABOVE LEFT) had a 3-liter six-cylinder engine with overhead valves operated by pushrods. The Harry Rush-designed Riley 11/40 Sports Model of 1922 (ABOVE) had a guaranteed top speed of 70mph and was commonly known as the "Redwing." The Duesenberg Model A Roadster (RIGHT) was advanced but very expensive. It had a straight-eight engine of 4.2 liters, and hydraulically operated front-wheel brakes.

vibration damper, the engine was said to be one of the smoothest-running of its time, and one of the most powerful, too. In its advertising Cord claimed no less than 265bhp at 4200rpm, although it's more likely that the engine's maximum output was actually nearer 200bhp. Either way, it gave the Model J stunning performance: it could reach 90mph in second gear and well over 100mph in top.

Auburn, too, produced a large flamboyant roadster absolutely typical of American sporting cars of the 1920s. Like Duesenberg, Auburn had been acquired by the dynamic EL Cord in the mid-1920s, and he soon set about revitalizing the company's entire range. The Auburn Speedster was introduced in 1928 with a 4.5-liter straight-eight engine by Lycoming developing about 90bhp, or a Lycoming V12 with which the car was guaranteed to exceed 100mph. The smaller-engined car had a two-speed rear axle which allowed effortless long-distance cruising on America's smooth, straight roads, but in Europe (where surprisingly large numbers of Auburns were sold) its soft suspension and vague, low-geared steering made it quite a handful to drive.

English manufacturers produced few genuine high-performance cars between the 1.5- and 4.5-liter classes during the 1920s. The nearest approach to the 2-liter models so popular on the Continent was probably the Lagonda 14/60 which appeared first in 1925, and then as the updated and improved Speed Model in 1927. With a

higher-compression engine set further back in the chassis and a close-ratio gearbox, this was good for 80mph and would run reliably at up to 4200rpm. In 1929 it gained a Cozette supercharger and, with 85bhp, would exceed 90mph. All Lagondas had excellent steering and handling characteristics.

French versions of the Italian fast 2-liter tourers were built along similar lines. They were somewhat heavier and less lively by virtue of their high gearing, but this made them ideal for long-distance cruising at about 60mph. The 2.2-liter 14/40 Delage appeared in 1921 with a side-valve engine, and until the 1928 launch of a range of six-cylinder engines it made a very pleasant fast tourer indeed. Also in France, Bignan built a four-valves-per-cylinder machine which won the 2-liter class in the 24-hour race at Spa in 1924, and in Grand Sport form this was a true 85mph car.

In technical terms, though, the most interesting sportscars of this period were undoubtedly the tiny French machines in the 1100cc class which, although available from the beginning of the 1920s, reached their heyday in about 1925. They varied widely in detail, but the basic formula was common to all: low weight (rarely much more than half a metric ton), high overall gearing, and tiny, high-revving engines with – for the time – very high specific power outputs. Two seats were the norm, but such was the cars' diminutive stature that often these were staggered slightly to provide a little more room for the driver's elbow.

Best-known of these so-called voiturettes was the Amilcar. This was originally intended to be an economy car, but in 1921 the company built a sports model almost as an afterthought, and this proved to be so popular that it entered production. There was nothing unduly remarkable about its side-valve engine and three-speed gearbox (apart from the former's incredibly primitive lubrication system) but it had an excellent chassis, and an Amilcar won the gruelling 24-hour Bol d'Or in 1922. This led to the development of the improved Grand Sport in 1923, and in this form the car began to be quite popular in Britain.

A twin-camshaft six-cylinder version appeared in 1925 – amazingly, still with only 1100cc – and in road trim was capable of 100mph. In racing, too, it was pretty well unbeatable, and not only won its class in the 200-mile races at Brooklands in 1926, 1927 and 1928, but in 1927 became the first 1100cc car to exceed 125mph on the road. An improved version of the Grand Sport was

The sleek metallic car (LEFT) is the Marendaz 9/90. Marendaz himself organized a number of energetic publicity stunts – this 1.1-liter from 1928 took a number of records at Monthléry as part of that program. The very first MG was a special-bodied Morris built by Cecil Kimber in 1925. Although not actually that first car, "Old Number One" (RIGHT) can be seen in the British Motor Industry Heritage Trust collection at Gaydon, Warwickshire.

launched in 1926 but by the end of the decade Amilcar was turning its attention toward luxurious small tourers and effectively abandoned sportscars.

The Amilcar and its French contemporaries – notably Lombard and Salmson – had no direct British counterparts but, in an even smaller class, high-performance versions of the famous Austin Seven were very popular. By as early as 1924 there was a pointed-tail Sports model which weighed in at well under half a metric ton – as, indeed, it had to for its 10bhp engine to produce anything like sporting performance. Maximum speed was, in fact, about 50mph. A supercharged Seven was added to the catalogue in 1928 and a year later the Ulster appeared which came with or without a supercharger. In this guise the engine would run at up to 5000rpm and the car was capable of at least 70mph.

The later 1920s also saw the advent of a name which, throughout the world, has been synonymous with sporting motoring ever since – Morris Garages or, as it was always better known, MG. Cecil Kimber began "manufacturing" cars in the early 1920s by the simple expedient of modifying standard Morris chassis and fitting them with his own bodywork, but it was the launch of the six-cylinder Morris Six in 1928 which led directly to the construction of the first true sportscar from MG. With a 2.5-liter overhead-camshaft engine and a three-speed gearbox, the so-called 18/80 was capable of around 75mph, and it was followed in 1930 by the Mark II with a better chassis, twin carburetors, a four-speed gearbox and servo-brakes. There was even a high-compression, dry-sumped Mark III, but only a handful of these were built.

The most famous early MG, however, was the M-type Midget. Based on the contemporary Morris Minor (which was itself, of course, a much more sophisticated rival to the Austin Seven), the 847cc Midget had a lively overhead-camshaft engine, a suitably lowered chassis, and lightweight two-seater bodywork; maximum speed was in the region of 60mph. It was the first cheap and reliable small British sportscar to provide performance which equalled the French 1100cc machines like the Amilcar, and it sold in large numbers.

Such was its success, in fact, that the MGs produced after World War II, like the TC, TD and TF, retained the M-type's vintage looks (this trend continued until as late as the mid-1950s in the case of the TF), and the Midget name was in use for an MG-badged car until as recently as 1980.

The American Essex (ABOVE LEFT) was introduced in 1919 with a 2.9-liter four-cylinder engine developing 55bhp which, in standard form, gave it a top speed of around 65mph. This modified car was photographed at the Shelsley Walsh hillclimb in July 1922. The Essex was popular in Britain because of its low price and relative sophistication. The 1920 GN Vitesse (LEFT) was sparsely equipped, even by cyclecar standards, but its light weight enabled its 1.1-liter air-cooled twin-cylinder engine to propel it at up to 65mph. A roller-bearing engine with chain-driven overhead camshafts followed in 1922. Motorcycle manufacturer Douglas built a number of light sportscars with 1.2-liter flat-twin air-cooled engines at the beginning of the 1920s, and, suitably tuned, they were often raced at Brooklands. This is a 1921 model (ABOVE). The 11.9hp Lagonda (RIGHT) was never listed as a sportscar, but it formed the basis of a modestly successful racing car.

The 1923 10.8hp Clyno Sports (LEFT) was renowned for its light, smooth steering and effective front-wheel brakes. Bodywork was aluminum and the 1.3-liter side-valve four-cylinder engine was mildy tuned. This early sporting Vauxhall is the delectable 1922 3-liter with Villiers supercharging (RIGHT). This 1923 "Duck's Back" Alvis 12/50 (MAIN PICTURE) was one of the most popular British sportscars of the 1920s.

Despite its somewhat staid appearance the Vauxhall 30/98 could achieve 85mph with ease, and racing versions were capable of a 100mph lap of Brooklands. The four-cylinder overhead-valve engine of the later OE models like this 1923 car (LEFT) developed 112bhp at 3500rpm. The air-cooled flat-twin ABC was initially little more than an economy light car with sporting pretensions, but the Super Sports which appeared in 1924 (RIGHT, FOREGROUND) had a slightly larger 1.3-liter engine and was capable of 70mph. Bamford and Martin built cars in west London from 1922 to 1925, the company later being renamed Aston Martin. This 1924 sports racing car (BELOW) featured a 1.5-liter four-cylinder engine with twin overhead camshafts and 16 valves.

The French Amilcar CS of the early 1920s (LEFT) had a four-cylinder, 1-liter side-valve engine and offered little more performance than most of its rivals. The 1924 CGS, however (BELOW LEFT), was an altogether different matter. It had only a slightly larger engine, but front-wheel brakes and semi-elliptic front springs made it a brisk performer. It was later developed into the lowered and more powerful CGSS "Surbaisse" model. The Bleriot Whippet (RIGHT) was a British cyclecar of conventional design, but with surprisingly good performance from its 1-liter twin-cylinder engine. The Mathis company made its name before World War I with its 1.3-liter Baby model, and for part of the 1920s it was the fourth-largest French car manufacturer after Citroën, Renault and Peugeot. The picture below shows two Mathises on the "Esses" in the 1924 Grand Prix de Tourisme at Lyon.

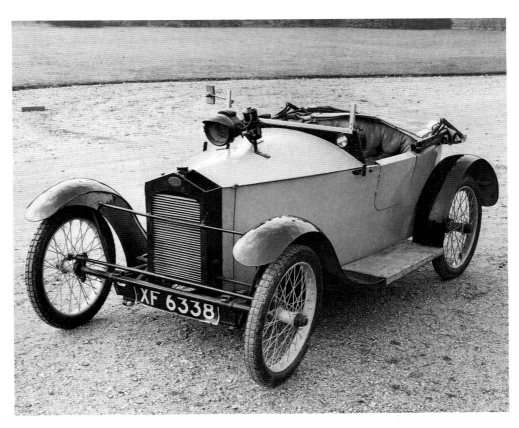

The first sporting Ballot was the 2-liter twin-cam of 1922 with four valves per cylinder. This was supplemented in 1923 by the 2LT tourer with a single overhead camshaft and only two valves per cylinder (LEFT). This 1924 model has a body by Lagache-Glaszman. The wonderfully named Chiribiri was an Italian design favoured by Nuvolari at the beginning of his career. This 1.5-liter car (MAIN PICTURE) has a body in the style of contemporary racing Fiats; the Englishman J E Scales is at the wheel. The DI was the mainstay of the Delage's important touring-car program from 1924 (RIGHT). It had a 2.1-liter, four-cylinder overhead-valve engine, a four-speed gearbox, a single-plate clutch and four-wheel brakes. This car has a body by Kelsch.

The Roaring Twenties 55

This 1920 Stutz Bearcat (LEFT) has the relatively unusual option of a full windshield and all-weather soft-top. Horstmann Cars Ltd of Bath in Somerset (now Avon) began building innovative light cars in 1914. Coventry-Simplex engines supplanted the original Horstmann unit in 1921 and at the same time a number of Sports and Super Sports models were announced. This car (BELOW) was photographed at the 200-Mile race at Brooklands in 1921 with T L Edwards at the wheel. The first Steyr appeared in 1920, designed by Hans Ledwinka. He left the company the following year, but all subsequent Steyrs, whether tourers, sportscars or racing cars, were based on his designs. This car (RIGHT) is shown at the 1922 Targa Florio.

The EHP was a conventional French voiturette of its period, often produced with closed bodywork rather than as a stark, open two-seater. A number of overhead-camshaft cars were built for racing, like this 1925 model (LEFT) with elegant wooden bodywork and a late-vintage 1750 Alfa Romeo engine. The driver in this photograph, probably taken in the 1960s, is P F Besley. The legendary Model T Ford, with a 2.9-liter four-cylinder engine, was in production from 1908 to 1927; more than 16 million were built. Most were rather plain but there were a few specials like this handsome 1922 Speedster (BELOW LEFT). The British HE had a 1.8-liter four-cylinder engine but this gave way to the 2-liter 14/20 tourer of 1920 and then to the sporting 14/40 (RIGHT), which had a close-ratio gearbox and a shorter chassis. The Aston Martin International (BELOW) began life in 1926. It was designed by A C Bertelli, with a 1.5-liter overhead-camshaft engine developing 50bhp, and a four-speed gearbox. A 63bhp dry-sump competition engine was announced in 1928, which helped the International enjoy a long and distinguished competition history.

The 2-liter six-cylinder 15/60 from OM (LEFT) was introduced in 1923 and later sports models were capable of 75mph. The car was extensively modified for the British market by the importers. It featured a 12-plug cylinder head, an ENV four-speed gearbox and Dewandre servo brakes. The Morgan RSS (Racing Super Sports) superseded the long-tailed Aero as the Morgan for serious competition (BELOW). This 1928 Blackburne-engined car has overhead valves and is capable of over 80mph. The standard Austin Seven tourer was developed into a number of nimble and surprisingly fast sports models. This Cozette-supercharged Super Sports (RIGHT) was introduced by Austin in 1928, and its 33bhp enabled it to exceed 70mph.

Triumph's 1929 Super Seven (LEFT) was distinguished by its hydraulic front brakes and three-bearing crankshaft, and was available with a Cozette supercharger if required. In spite of the narrowness and height of its bodywork the 1.5-liter Cozette-supercharged Lea-Francis Hyper (BELOW LEFT) was a very rapid car; a Hyper, driven by Kaye Don, won the first Ulster Tourist Trophy race. The 1929 Austin Ulster (RIGHT) was among the most exotic of the high-performance Austin Seven variants. It featured a lowered front axle, close-ratio gearbox, pressure-fed lubrication, and a top speed in excess of 70mph. The 1.1-liter Vernon Derby (BELOW) was one of the better-finished French voiturettes, but it never achieved the same popularity as the Amilcar and Salmson. The car shown here is a 1929 model.

The French-built front-wheel-drive Tracta (LEFT) was designed by J A Grégoire. Front suspension was by sliding pillars, and the four-speed gearbox was mounted forward of the engine. This 1.5-liter sports model, capable of over 80mph, was photographed in about 1929. The Arab (RIGHT) was a handsome sportscar designed by Reid Railton. It appeared in 1926 with a 2-liter engine and four-wheel brakes, but such was Railton's disillusionment after the tragic death in 1927 of his mentor, Parry Thomas, that the project was abandoned soon afterwards. The Frazer Nash (BELOW) retained the dog-clutch-and-chain transmission of the GN and this, coupled to its light weight, made it a very fast car for its time. This is a 1.5-liter sports tourer; there were also several models for serious competition work.

66 The Sportscar Album

Launched in 1928, the Duesenberg Model J was bigger, faster, more elaborate and more expensive than almost anything else then available in America, and it also set new standards of refinement and appearance. Its 6.9-liter straight-eight engine featured twin overhead camshafts operating four valves per cylinder, and despite its weight it was capable of at least 116mph. Above is a 1929 Model J convertible coupe; above right is a 1929 convertible roadster with a Murphy body. Scarcely less elegant was the 1929 Dupont Model G Speedster (LEFT). The 5.3-liter side-valve straight-eight gave a guaranteed 100mph. Pierce-Arrow enjoyed a long and distinguished career among prestige American car-builders, although the company was under the control of Studebaker by the time this 1929 long-chassis Eight convertible (RIGHT) was built.

68 The Sportscar Album

The lowered chassis and cycle-type wings make the Amilcar CGSS (LEFT) look a much more modern car than it really was. The 1.1-liter four-cylinder side-valve engine developed 35bhp and the little car was very popular in England until it was ousted by home-produced cars like the MG Midget and Riley Nine. Cottin-Desgouttes cars were frequent entrants in French sports- and touring-car events. The car shown here (MAIN PICTURE) is a 1925 4-liter with a later body by Offord. Looking not unlike a scaled-down Bentley, the Marendaz Special (RIGHT) was typical of between-the-wars British sportscars. The 1926 car shown here has a 1.5-liter side-valve Anzani engine.

The Roaring Twenties 69

In addition to its elegant roadsters Delage built a number of six-cylinder tourers like this 1929 car (LEFT). The Type 23 "Brescia" Bugatti was named after the Italian town where a win in the 1921 voiturette race helped re-establish the company's reputation after World War I. Engines were available with two or four valves per cylinder. This tourer (BELOW) dates from 1925. There were many small sportscar manufacturers in France after World War I and the two best-known were Amilcar and Salmson: the latter building this Grand Sport (RIGHT) in 1929. The 1.1-liter four-cylinder engine had twin overhead camshafts and from 1926 all sports models had cowled radiators and front-wheel brakes. Salmsons were usually cheaper than Amilcars, but the powerful twin-plug supercharged San Sebastian was considerably faster.

72 The Sportscar Album

The Type 43 (LEFT) was launched in 1927 and was capable of over 100mph thanks to a supercharged 2.3-liter engine. The pre-1914 Prince Henry Austro-Daimler is regarded as one of the first genuine sportscars. This 1927 3-liter single-overhead-camshaft 19/100 (MAIN PICTURE) has two-seater coachwork from Vanden Plas. The elegant 1.75-liter Alfa Romeo 1750 (RIGHT) from 1929 was fast and controllable, and it gained a great reputation in the Mille Miglia, Targa Florio and Irish Grand Prix.

The Roaring Twenties 73

Chapter FOUR

From Austerity to Luxury

In the immediate postwar period, the austere economic conditions in Europe favored the manufacture of sober sedans and light commercial vehicles rather than frivolous sports models. Yet a surprising number of sportscars did go into production in the five year period between 1945 and 1950.

The large sportscar of the 1930s was dead, however. In a Germany struggling to revive its motor industry, there could be no question of building cars like the big Mercedes roadsters of the previous decade. In Italy, the market for cars like the Alfa-Romeo 2900C had disappeared. And in France, a taxation system biased heavily against large-capacity engines prevented the effective revival of the *grandes routières* of the 1930s.

Nevertheless, motoring enjoyment had not disappeared. Obliged to export in order to survive, MG in Britain found that a market still existed for small and affordable sportscars. The 1945 TC model which was used to exploit this market was a revived 1930s design; a crude four-cylinder roadster which could manage just 78mph but was cheap to buy, cheap to run, and offered open-air fun. Its success outside Britain – and particularly in the US – helped to establish the British-style roadster as a popular sportscar norm which would be respected worldwide for more than 20 years.

One level above the MG, the prewar BMW 328 had created a new type of fast and civilized sportscar. Unable to restart production before 1950, the German company saw its initiative picked up by Jaguar in the 1948 XK120, a remarkable two-seater with BMW-inspired styling and a brand-new 160bhp DOHC six-cylinder engine originally designed for the forthcoming Jaguar sedan. With 120mph performance and a price tag which made it accessible to middle-class motorists, the XK120 sold very well indeed and established Jaguar's reputation in the US. The BMW influence was seen elsewhere, too: in the small-volume Frazer Nash models (Frazer Nash had been BMW's British importer in the 1930s); and in the Bristol, although the latter was a sports sedan rather than a true sportscar.

The late 1940s also saw several new hopefuls start up in business, creating sporting chassis and bodywork around mechanical elements bought from the major manufacturers. In Britain, the Healey combined lightness, good aerodynamics and a four-cylinder Riley engine to achieve 106mph in 1946, while the Allard's spirited acceleration and 98mph top speed came from its side-valve Ford V8. By 1950, Ford-engined Allards could reach 115mph. In Italy, Fiat engines went into small sportscars from Cisitalia, Osca and others. Yet all these models were built in small numbers.

From Austerity to Luxury 135

PREVIOUS PAGE: This 1950 short-chassis version of Ferrari's 166 had open bodywork by Touring. The engine was a 140bhp 2-liter V12.

LEFT: The Jaguar XK120 was introduced in 1948 and had an enormous impact on the sportscar market. Its 3.4-liter twin-cam six-cylinder engine offered affordable 120mph motoring. This 1952 example has non-standard Borrani wire wheels.

ABOVE: Many manufacturers entered the postwar period with revived prewar models. One such was MG, whose characterful 1250cc TC model was very similar to 1939's TB.

RIGHT: Triumph entered the sportscar fray in 1953 with the TR2, which changed the face of the cheap sportscar market with its modern styling. Its 2-liter engine gave 100 mph performance.

From Austerity to Luxury 137

LEFT: Chevrolet's 1953 Corvette is instantly recognizable with its long, low body and racy lines. As there was no possibility of developing a new engine for such a low-production-run car, it initially came with Chevrolet's existing 150bhp straight-six engine, but later models all had V8 engines. This is a 1954 car.

RIGHT: The Porsche 356 was based on Volkswagen mechanical elements, and by 1955, this gorgeous Speedster version was capable of 120mph with an engine capacity of just 1582cc.

Ultimately, the most successful of the new Italian sportscar makers was Ferrari. Its founder – a former racing driver and manager of the Alfa-Romeo team – built his own chassis and engines, and used specialist coachbuilders for the bodywork. The first Ferrari on sale to the public was the 1949 Tipo 166, which gave awesome performance from its 140bhp 2-liter V12 engine. Rare and expensive, it set the tone for all future Ferrari models.

During the 1950s, the shape of the popular sportscar changed dramatically, although small-volume Morgan in Britain persisted with its individualistic 1930s-style roadsters. The abilities of the popular sportscar also changed almost beyond recognition, and by the end of the decade, 100mph maximum speeds, safe handling and good brakes were the norm.

Probably the most important new model was the 1953 Triumph TR2, which was introduced into the popular sportscar market primarily to compete with MG in the US. It offered much more performance than the contemporary MG TD, together with a streamlined, full-width body style which made the MG's wings and running boards look old-fashioned overnight. Not until 1955 did MG retaliate with the MGA, a much prettier but still rather slower car than the Triumph. Together with the Austin Healey, the MG and the Triumph offered a simplicity and ruggedness which appealed greatly to Americans, and their sales earned large export revenues for Britain.

By contrast, the popular Italian sportscars did not fare so well abroad. They were perceived as fragile, largely because of their high-revving, small-capacity engines: typical were Alfa Romeo's 1955 Giulietta coupe, which managed over 100mph from just 1,290cc, and the later 120mph lightweight Zagato-bodied SZ coupe which had an uprated version of the same engine. Even the larger-capacity Alfas, with twin-cam 2-liter engines, were barely faster. Yet simplicity and ruggedness were not everything; dealer support was also crucial. The revolutionary Lotus Elite was a fine-handling car and the world's first all-fiberglass monocoque, yet it foundered in the US because it lacked a dealer network.

The American domestic manufacturers had nothing to challenge the imported sportscars. It was General Motors which first tried, with its 1953 Chevrolet Corvette. To keep prices down at Triumph and MG levels, the Corvette used mechanical elements from existing sedans in a new fiberglass body, the first ever seen on a series-production car. Many of the Corvette's features (such as its standard two-speed automatic transmission) were typically American; straight-line performance was excellent, but sharp handling was sacrificed for a boulevard ride. The Corvette failed to stem the tide of British sportscar imports, but it did create a new market for an all-American sportscar.

The basic shape of the Corvette underwent various alterations over the decade, and power and performance increased dramatically. By 1960, the optional

315bhp V8 engine put 130mph within reach. Even other US manufacturers were unable to compete. Ford tried in 1955 with its Thunderbird, very much a Corvette competitor rather than a challenger to the British imports, but after 1957 the model put on weight and size and settled into a different market niche.

The most successful middle-class sportscar maker of the 1950s was Jaguar. From 1951, it offered a fixed-head version of its XK120 alongside the open car, and there would be both open and closed versions of the XK140 (1955) and XK150 (1957). These later models continued the XK120 theme, but embodied improvements tested in Jaguar's racing program which gave them qualities unique at the price. By the end of the decade, the XK150 was capable of more than 130mph and had rack-and-pinion steering together with disk brakes on its front wheels. Many higher-priced cars were barely faster and still made do with vague recirculating-ball steering and fade-prone drum brakes.

Yet Jaguar did not have things all its own way in the mid-priced sportscar market. After 1950, it faced competition from the German Porsche 356, and after 1955 from the Mercedes-Benz 190SL. The rear-engined Porsche was the cheaper of the two, and was available only as a closed coupe before 1955. Its top speed was little better than that of a Triumph TR and its handling could surprise the unwary, but it had considerable driver appeal. From 1955, a 120mph four-cam Carrera version was available, and this was further uprated in 1958. Worldwide, sales volumes were similar to Jaguar's, and the 356 models established a formidable reputation for their makers.

The Mercedes was slightly more expensive than the Porsche. Its performance was broadly similar to that of the cheaper Triumph TR, but its specification incorporated several technical advances. While other sportscars had a separate chassis to give rigidity to their open bodies, the 190SL had a strong unitary body shell, and while other sportscars had crude beam axles and semi-elliptic leaf springs at the rear, the Mercedes had an independent swing-axle rear suspension with coil springs. Also unusual in its class was the option of servo-assisted brakes, which became standard in 1957.

At the very top of the market, the Spanish truck manufacturer Pegaso announced a quad-cam V8 Coupe with a five-speed transaxle and the option of a supercharger, but was unable to sell many examples. In France, Facel Vega attempted to revive the *grande routière* tradition in 1954 with a striking 130mph sports coupe powered by an American Chrysler V8 engine. In Britain, Aston Martin entered the fray with the DB2 in 1950, developing this progressively until the 140mph DB4 was ready to replace it in 1958. The DB4's happy combination of Italian styling with British engineering established Aston Martin firmly in the supercar league.

Ferrari offered its first series-production car, the 250GT, in 1956; this coupe usually came with a body by Pininfarina. By the end of the decade, some versions of the Ferrari V12 engine gave as much as 340bhp, and maximum speeds were around 140mph. After 1958, these speeds were matched by Maserati's 3500GT, the first road-going car from the established Italian racing car manufacturer. But the best-remembered exotic sportscar of the period is undoubtedly Mercedes' 300SL, notable for its pioneering use of fuel injection, its space-frame construction, and its distinctive "gullwing" doors. With the right gearing, this 195bhp coupe was capable of well over 150mph as early as 1954. Most versions were geared for around 135mph, however, and the later roadster derivative was a less individualistic car.

LEFT: By the time this DB4 drophead was built in the early 1960s, Aston Martin's twin-cam 3.6-liter engine was giving 140mph performance. Sadly, Astons were beyond the range of all but the very wealthy.

ABOVE RIGHT: The fabulous "Gullwing" Mercedes-Benz 300SL was so named after its upward-opening doors. Developed from a works competition car, it could achieve 150mph with the right gearing.

RIGHT: Jaguar's XK range was developed during the 1950s, and by 1960, when this XK150 was built, it had 3.8 liters and up to 265bhp.

From Austerity to Luxury 139

LEFT: The British HRG was another car which carried on the traditions of the 1930s. This 1948 1500 model, with Singer engine, only gave around 80mph, but what it lacked in performance, it certainly made up for in style.

RIGHT: Many people thought of the 1947 Rover 12hp Tourer as a sportscar, although it was really too much of a family model to justify such a description. Again, prewar styling is in evidence.

BELOW: Triumph's first attempt at a sportscar was not a great success: the 1800 model was introduced in 1946 and was too cumbersome to be really sporting.

From Austerity to Luxury 143

LEFT: Bristol's 400 was an expensive handbuilt sports sedan based heavily on prewar BMW designs, but it was notable for its aluminum body and aerodynamic shape.

BELOW LEFT: Only 15 examples of the first postwar Aston Martin, the DB1, were built. The styling was not as successful as that of later Astons, but the essential ingredient of high performance was already there.

RIGHT: Sydney Allard's 1946 K1 model looked like a prewar trials special but offered astonishing acceleration from its Ford V8 engine. Later cars had even more powerful American V8s.

BELOW: MG updated its 1250cc TC for 1950 to make the TD. It sold very well outside its native Britain, even though many elements of the design were anachronistic.

Jaguar developed the XK120 theme to produce several different models, but the success of all of them was largely based on the brilliant twin-overhead-camshaft XK engine developed by William Heynes in 1948. The picture on the left shows a 1953 fixed-head coupe version, below is a 1949 roadster, and on the right is a 1954 drophead coupe. The roadsters were the most numerous variant, though very few had the lightweight aluminum body panels of the car pictured. This car is one of the first 240 which were built in this way before unexpected demand led to a "production" steel-bodied version. Fixed-head coupes were the next most popular, while the drophead coupe did not appear until 1953 and is consequently quite rare.

From Austerity to Luxury 147

LEFT: Riley's sedan-derived 2½-liter roadster was an unsuccessful attempt to produce a long-distance sporting tourer for the US market.

BELOW LEFT: Sunbeam's Alpine was based on the earlier Sunbeam-Talbot 90. This 1955 model had a 2.3-liter four-cylinder engine giving 95mph.

RIGHT: The Austin Healey had a reputation as a real man's sportscar. This is a six-cylinder 100/6 model of the late 1950s, with 108mph top speed.

BELOW: Before selling his new design to Austin, Donald Healey built his own sportscars. Most charismatic of all was the Healey Silverstone, a thinly-disguised sports-racer with Riley 2½-liter engine and 107mph top speed.

ABOVE: The Talbot-Lago Grand Sport was a strikingly attractive French-built car. The 4.4-liter six-cylinder engine gave 190bhp. This is a 1949 Le Mans coupe version.

LEFT: The French Delahaye firm was unable to sell enough of its exotic sports models to survive beyond 1953. This is a 1952 type 235, with 3557cc six-cylinder engine and coupe body by Figoni and Falaschi.

RIGHT: This 1952 Allard J2X represents the marque's later American-engined models. Like the Healey Silverstone, it was a roadgoing sports racer.

From Austerity to Luxury 151

ABOVE LEFT: The 1956 second-generation Chevrolet Corvette brought in attractive two-tone finishes and more chrome. Bodies were still made of fiberglass, but all engines were now the famous smallblock V8, which was successfully wedded to the Corvette by Zora Arkus Duntov.

LEFT: A 1957 Corvette roadster with striking two-tone paint, seen against a California sunset.

ABOVE: Ford's answer to the Corvette was the Thunderbird. This 1956 car had the hardtop option and a V8 engine.

RIGHT: Pininfarina designed the attractive body on this 1955 Lancia B24 Spyder. Its 2½-liter V6 engine gave 112mph performance.

ABOVE: The British Kieft 1100 sports racer saw small-volume production between 1954 and 1956. Its 1098cc Coventry-Climax engine gave 110mph plus.

LEFT: The "supercar" 300SL Mercedes evolved from gullwing coupe to stylish roadster in 1957. Most examples were geared for around 125mph.

RIGHT: The 1956 250GT had a 2953cc V12 engine and was Ferrari's first volume-produced model. This one is a competition coupe version with Scaglietti-built body to a Pininfarina design.

RIGHT: Abarth's Fiat-based cars earned a formidable reputation in the 1950s. This 747cc Zagato-bodied coupe with the "double bubble" roof was good for 95mph.

LEFT: The exotic low-volume Pegaso was Spain's only sportscar. Around 100 were built between 1951 and 1956, all with complex quad-cam V8 engines.

BELOW: The third-generation Chevrolet Corvette lasted from 1958 to 1962. This is one of the earlier examples, with a 4.6-liter V8 engine.

ABOVE: The 1956 BMW 507 never matched the success of Mercedes' 300SL models, but its 3168cc V8 and shapely body made a heady cocktail.

LEFT: One of Alfa Romeo's enduring classics was the 1954 Giulietta Sprint coupe, with beautiful Bertone styling and 100mph from its twin-cam 1290cc engine.

ABOVE RIGHT: Another enduring Italian classic was the Pininfarina-styled Lancia Aurelia GT, introduced in 1953. This is a 1957 model, with 2½-liter V6 engine and 112mph performance.

RIGHT: Zagato styled the 1963 Alfa Romeo TZ sports racer, which had a backbone chassis and could reach 133mph with just 1.6 liters.

158 The Sportscar Album

ABOVE: The French-built Salmson 2300S coupe had an all-alloy 2.3-liter engine which gave 110mph. This example dates from 1955.

LEFT: Jowett's 1950 Jupiter had a 1486cc flat-four engine. Its 85mph performance did not promote large sales and it was withdrawn in 1954.

ABOVE RIGHT: The 100S was the rare alloy-bodied competition version of the four-cylinder Austin-Healey. This one was built in 1955.

RIGHT: The 1954 AC Ace's elderly six-cylinder engine let down an otherwise remarkable car with all-independent suspension and stunning good looks.

These are later variants of Jaguar's immortal XK range. The XK140 replaced the XK120 in 1955, and is seen (LEFT) in roadster form. The XK150 with straight-through wing lines arrived in 1957, and from 1958 the more powerful XK150S model was made available, alongside the standard type, to accommodate the extra weight that the XK range was putting on. The twin-cam 3.8-liter engines in the 1959 XK150S fixed-head coupe (BELOW) and 1960 drophead coupe (RIGHT) gave 130mph performance.

162 The Sportscar Album

LEFT: The Aceca was the fixed-head coupe version of AC's Ace, and was introduced in 1955 with the same 2-liter six-cylinder engine as the open car.

BELOW: Bristol's 1954 404 was known as the Businessman's Express. It was an expensive, hand-built coupe capable of 110mph. Just 44 examples were built.

RIGHT: The 1954 Swallow Doretti used Triumph TR mechanical elements but its refinements added weight which in turn sapped performance. Only 250 were made.

BELOW RIGHT: The MGA sold strongly in the later 1950s. This is a 1600 Mk II model of the early 1960s, which just exceeded 100mph on 1622cc.

From Austerity to Luxury 163

LEFT: The first "production" Lotus was the Seven, announced in 1957. Its light weight permitted startling performance from a variety of humble family sedan engines.

BELOW: The Austin-Healey 100/6 could be had as a two-seater or as a 2+2. This 1958 BN4 model has the two occasional seats installed.

RIGHT: 1958's small Austin-Healey was called the "frogeye" because of its headlamp arrangement. It managed 83mph from its 948cc four-cylinder engine.

From Austerity to Luxury 167

LEFT: Fastest of the MGAs was the 1958 Twin-Cam, with 1588cc and twin overhead camshafts. Center-lock wheels and disk brakes were standard.

TOP: The 1958 Lotus Elite offered a brilliant combination of handling, road-holding and 112mph performance in a glass-fiber monocoque shell.

ABOVE: To get 123mph from their big 541R coupe of 1957, Jensen employed Austin's 3993cc straight-six from the A135 limousine.

Chapter FIVE

The Swinging Sixties

Among popular and mid-priced European sportscars of the 1960s, front engines, rear-wheel-drive and four-speed gearboxes were still the norm, although all-synchromesh boxes had generally replaced the crash-first type common in the 1950s. By the end of the decade, the five-speed gearbox - more or less exclusive to Italian manufacturers in the 1950s – was beginning to gain ground, and it was no longer unusual for automatic transmission to be an easily available option.

Alone among the makers of popular models, Lancia tried front-wheel-drive on its 1965 Fulvia coupe, an attractive car which went on to sell in large volumes. Porsche persevered with its rear-mounted engines and, at the top of the market, a number of mid-engined, small-volume exotics arrived towards the end of the decade. The mid-engine position, inspired by earlier racing car practice, gave better weight distribution and therefore better handling, although it also made passenger and luggage accommodation marginal. Only Lotus tried it further down the market, with the 1966 Europa.

At the beginning of the decade, popular sportscars almost without exception had beam rear axles, and the first newcomers followed the tradition of the 1950s. Thus, MG's new MGB arrived in 1961 with a beam axle on semi-elliptic leaf springs, and soon began to look outdated. Not that this hindered its popularity at all, for the "B" went on to become MG's best-selling model ever.

Things soon began to change, however. Triumph's cheap and cheerful new Spitfire of 1962 had a swing-axle rear end (inherited from the Herald sedan it was based on), and the larger Triumph TRs took on a semi-trailing arm independent rear end in 1964 – though not for the US, where such systems were still mistrusted. Fiat's lovely 124 Spyder, introduced in 1966 and aimed mainly at the US market, recognized this mistrust and clung to an old-fashioned beam axle. Jaguar, however, had committed themselves to a complicated but extremely effective independent rear end for their 1961 E-type, and Mercedes-Benz persevered with their swing-axles, improving the layout for the new 230SL which they introduced in 1963.

Disk brakes also gained ground during the 1960s, and by the end of the decade, there were no sportscars in production which did not have them on the front wheels at least. Many had them all round: the 1961 E-type Jaguar, the 1963 Mercedes SL and the 1966 Alfa Romeo Duetto represented the trend. Rack-and-pinion steering, too, took over from earlier types, adding a welcome precision to the handling which was often complemented by radial-ply tires.

As in the 1950s, both closed and open sportscars

PREVIOUS PAGE: The unforgettable E-type Jaguar was introduced in 1961. This 1963 4.2-liter Series I roadster shows the sensuous styling which gave these 150mph cars so much of their appeal.

LEFT: The rear-engined Porsche 911 of 1964 was an exhilarating performer. Descendants of the car remain in production today, nearly 30 years later.

ABOVE RIGHT: One of the best-loved 1960s sportscars was the MGB, which was in production for 17 years. This is a 1972 roadster model, with a 1798cc four-cylinder engine which gave around 105mph.

RIGHT: America still loved its Corvettes in the 1960s. These are fourth-generation Sting Ray models with brutally powerful V8 engines.

proved popular, and most makers of open models hedged their bets either by offering a closed coupe variant or a removable hardtop, the latter often made of fiberglass in order to save weight. The Mercedes SL came with both convertible top and steel hardtop as standard from the beginning, and Triumph introduced the so-called "Surrey top" as an option on its 1961 TR4, which combined a fixed rear window section with removable fabric or metal roof panels. Porsche developed this idea further as the "Targa top" in 1967, this time combining a removable roof panel with a foldaway soft-top containing the rear window.

Right at the top of the market, however, the closed sportscar reigned supreme. One reason was the need for extra body rigidity in a very high-performance car, but another and equally important one was that customers were becoming increasingly conscious of the discomfort of open-air motoring at very high speeds and of the attendant safety risks.

Safety in car design had become an issue in the US in the mid-1960s, and every manufacturer who wanted to sell cars there was eventually obliged to conform to new safety standards introduced in 1968. Even before the introduction of these new standards, however, the US sportscar market had gone its own sweet way. US customers continued to buy European models in quantity from MG, Triumph, Jaguar, Mercedes-Benz, Fiat and Alfa Romeo, but they also supported the very different offerings from domestic manufacturers. Ford scored a major success with the Mustang "ponycar" in

1964, pricing it between the MGB and Triumph TR4. General Motors responded with the Chevrolet Camaro in 1966, while continuing to develop the Corvette. And for those who wanted straight-line performance above all else, there were the "musclecars" – essentially stripped-out sedans with enormously powerful engines but questionable brakes and handling.

The most popular sportscars of the decade came from Britain and from Germany, while American sportscars still meant very little outside the US even though they sold in huge numbers at home. The most significant Europeans were the MGB, the Jaguar E-type, the Mercedes-Benz 230/250/280SL and the Porsche 911, while the US market was dominated by Ford's Mustang and Chevrolet's Corvette and Camaro. In Europe, Ferrari and Aston Martin continued to build on their already solid reputations, but sales volumes were low at their end of the market.

The MGB was significant mainly because it was the archetypal cheap sportscar, rapid without being really fast in standard form, simple to maintain, and endowed with enduring good looks. The E-type Jaguar offered stunning performance (though the claimed 150mph was not available on standard models) and a beautiful shape. In Germany, the Mercedes SL took the concept of the civilized sportscar a stage further, while the 1964 Porsche 911 had exhilarating performance and rewarding handling (for those drivers who got it right). The successful US sports models, by contrast, depended almost entirely on straight-line performance.

LEFT: Ferrari still favored V12 engines in the 1960s, and the twin-overhead-camshaft, dry-sump type is fitted to this 1967 275GTB4 model. The engine displaced 3286cc, and could produce up to 300bhp. The car was capable of 165mph, and the lovely coupe body was built by Scaglietti to a design by the famous Italian styling firm, Pininfarina.

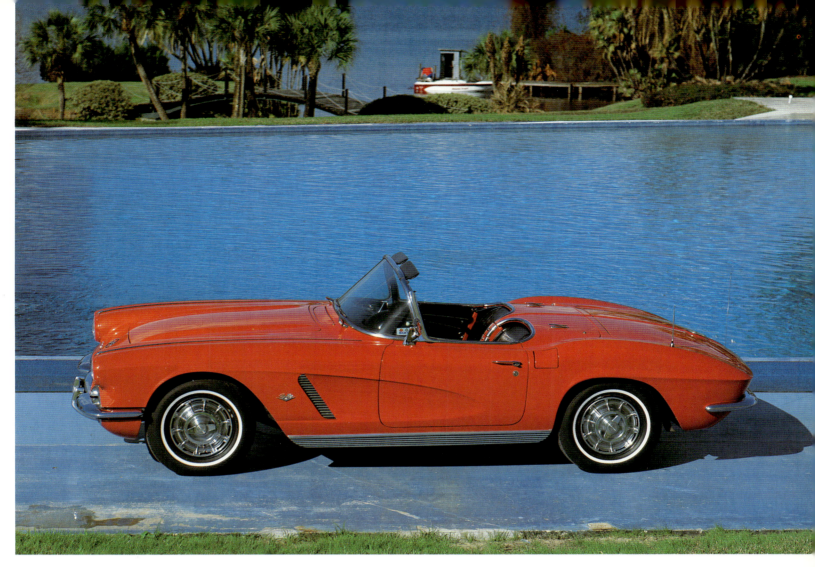

ABOVE LEFT: The 190SL Mercedes-Benz was a more affordable, 106mph, companion model to the 300SL. It was made from 1955 to 1963, and the cars pictured here are 1960 models.

LEFT: Porsche's RS60 Spyder was a sports-racer which saw only limited production. This example dates from 1960.

ABOVE: The last of the third-generation Chevrolet Corvettes had the so-called "ducktail" rear end. This 1962 model had a 5.3-liter V8 engine.

RIGHT: The last of Porsche's 356 models was made in 1965. This is a rare 1964 Carrera 2, with a four-cam 2-liter flat-four engine which gave a top speed of 125mph.

176 The Sportscar Album

LEFT: TVR introduced their Grantura coupe in 1958. This is a 1962 Mk III, which had the MGA's 1622cc engine and could exceed 100mph.

RIGHT: Daimler's only sportscar was the glass-fiber bodied SP250 of 1959, which had 120mph performance from its refined 2½-liter V8 engine.

BELOW: The big Austin-Healeys took on BMC's latest 2.9-liter engine in 1959, and were rechristened 3000 models. This is a 1961 example.

The Swinging Sixties 177

TOP: The Lotus Elite was gradually improved, and this 1962 Series II model had better trim and a better rear suspension than the original cars.

ABOVE: The Ogle SX1000 was a short-lived sports coupe with glass-fiber body and Mini mechanical elements. Just 66 were made between 1962 and 1964.

RIGHT: Aston Martin's short-chassis DB4 became a DB4GT sports racer when fitted in 1960 with lightweight Zagato coachwork. The resulting performance from the 314bhp engine was electrifying.

Still a beautiful-looking car, the Jaguar E-type remains a symbol of high-performance motoring more than 30 years after its 1961 introduction. The original models (MAIN PICTURE) had the 3.8-liter version of the twin-cam six-cylinder XK engine. From 1964 (BELOW LEFT), cars had a 4.2-liter engine with improved torque characteristics. The E-type came as a roadster, a fixed-head coupe or (from 1966 to 1968) a rather bloated 2+2 coupe. A V12 engine replaced the six for the 1970s.

TOP: The Aston Martin DB5 sports sedan was available between 1964 and 1965, and promised 140mph from its twin-cam 4-liter engine.

ABOVE: Dropping a 4.2-liter American Ford V8 into the Sunbeam Alpine roadster in 1964 created the 120mph Sunbeam Tiger.

RIGHT: The AC Cobra was another high-performance cross-breed; a British AC Ace with the 4.7-liter V8 from the Ford Mustang under its hood. The red car (ABOVE RIGHT) is a 1964 Le Mans version; the blue roadster (BELOW RIGHT) is a 1966 Mk III model. Only 560 4.7-liter "289" Cobras were built.

LEFT: The Sunbeam Alpine was an affordable 1725cc sportscar of the 1960s which failed to become as popular as its MG and Triumph rivals.

BELOW LEFT: The Reliant Scimitar had an Ogle-designed body made of glass-fibre and clothing Ford running gear. It managed 117mph from 2½ liters.

RIGHT: The 1962 Triumph Spitfire was a popular and affordable sportscar. Its 1147cc Herald sedan engine would take the car beyond 90mph.

BELOW: By contrast, the Alvis TF21 was an expensive bespoke sports sedan, with a 3-liter six under the hood and 120mph top speed. This is a 1966 car.

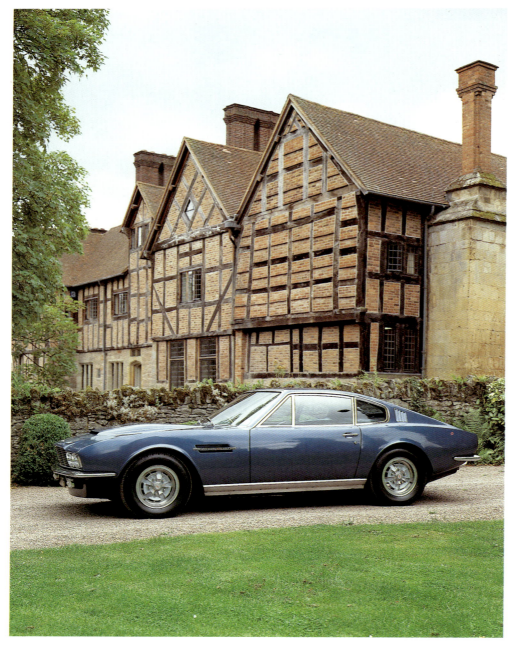

TOP LEFT: Triumph's TRs gained Italian body styling in 1961 and independent rear suspension in 1964. This is a 1967 TR4A, which has both features.

ABOVE: The MG Midget of 1961 was a badge-engineered Mk II Austin-Healey Sprite. The first ones had 948cc engines, but later cars like this 1968 model had 1098cc types.

LEFT: Aston Martin's 5.3-liter quad-cam V8 became available in the DBS models in 1969. In fuel-injected form, it made the cars capable of 160mph.

RIGHT: Last of the old-style Astons was the DB6, with a 4-liter straight six and 148mph top speed. Production came to an end in 1971.

LEFT: BMC replaced the big Austin-Healeys with a six-cylinder derivative of the MGB called the MGC in 1967. Neither performance nor handling was up to scratch and the car was not a success.

BELOW LEFT: Both four-cylinder MGB and six-cylinder MGC came as roadsters or as "GT" coupes. This is a 1969 MGB roadster.

ABOVE LEFT: The Bond Equipe had glass-fiber coupe or convertible bodies on Triumph Vitesse running gear. The engine in this 1969 example is a 2-liter straight-six.

ABOVE RIGHT: The Gilbern Genie of the late 1960s also had a glass-fiber body and bought-in engine – in this case a Ford 2½-liter or 3-liter V6.

BELOW: There was only a Ford 1600 four-cylinder in the 1967 TVR Vixen, but the glass-fiber coupe could top 100mph. Later cars, like this one, reached 110mph.

LEFT: Scaglietti built the Pininfarina-styled body on the stunning Ferrari 250GTO of 1962. It was all but unbeatable in sportscar races of the time.

ABOVE: The short-wheelbase version of the Ferrari 250GT was known as the 250GT Berlinetta. This is a 1960 model, finished in the Italian racing red so beloved of Ferrari enthusiasts.

RIGHT: Small-volume British manufacturer Marcos used laminated plywood construction and small Ford engines for its GT model. This is a 1960 example.

LEFT: The 1962 Iso Rivolta GT coupe had bodywork by Bertone and a 5.3-liter Chevrolet V8 engine which offered 140mph performance.

BELOW: The 1963 Vallelunga was De Tomaso's first roadgoing car, and depended for its performance on an American Ford V8. The body was by Ghia.

RIGHT: Maserati built their own engines – twin-cam straight-sixes for the 1964 Mistral, which had body styling by Frua.

BELOW RIGHT: Even lowly Fiats could have high-class bodies. In the case of the 1965 850 Spyder, the styling was by Bertone. Around 95mph was possible from the rear-mounted 843cc (later 903cc) engine.

The Swinging Sixties 195

LEFT: The 275-series Ferraris had 3.3-liter V12 engines. This is a 1965 275GTB "shortnose" car, styled by Pininfarina. Top speed was around 150mph.

ABOVE: Lamborghini presented a credible threat to Ferrari's supremacy in Italy with cars like the 1966 Miura, with a quad-cam V12 which gave 170mph.

CENTER RIGHT: From 1964, the 330-series Ferraris presented yet another V12, this time a 4-liter type. This 1967 330GTC is based on the short-chassis 275GTB.

BOTTOM RIGHT: One of the most beautiful of all Ferraris was 1968's 365GTB4 "Daytona", with a 4.9-liter, dry-sump, quad-cam V12 giving 352bhp.

196   The Sportscar Album

The Swinging Sixties 197

FAR LEFT: The Volvo P1800 used its maker's bullet-proof B18 sedan engine in an attractive coupe body built in Britain. When body assembly reverted to Sweden, the car was redesignated a P1800S.

LEFT: The Panhard 24BT of the mid-1960s was an oddball French coupe, which managed nearly 100mph with a 60bhp, 845cc flat-twin engine.

RIGHT: The Matra Djet was another intriguing French coupe, which offered both good looks and sporting performance from its 1-liter engine.

BELOW: In the US, Ford introduced the enormously successful Mustang in 1964. Not all versions offered as much performance as this 1966 model with its big 4.7-liter V8 engine, however.

The Swinging Sixties 199

American sportscars of the 1960s were characterized by engines which were sometimes brutally powerful. The Ford GT40 (TOP LEFT) was a limited-production road racer, with a mid-mounted V8 in its British-built body. The Shelby Mustang GT 350 (LEFT) was a high-performance version of Ford's best-seller tuned by Carroll Shelby. Above is the Chevrolet Corvette Sting Ray, while below left is a 1967 Chevrolet Camaro with the top-option Z28 performance package. The Pontiac Firebird (BELOW RIGHT) was a Camaro derivative.

LEFT: Mercedes-Benz sports models of the 1960s depended as much on refinement as on high performance. This 1968 "pagoda-roof" 280SL had a 2.8-liter straight-six which gave it a 120mph top speed.

BELOW: The end of the 1960s saw the arrival of a restyled Ford Mustang, seen here in 1969 "Mach 1" high-performance coupe guise.

RIGHT: The fifth-generation Chevrolet Corvette was announced in 1968. Engine options were all V8s, ranging in power from 300bhp up to 435bhp.

Chapter SIX

From Musclecar to Crisis

The sportscar market changed radically once again in the 1970s, though not because of innovations in engineering. The forces for change were external; on the one hand, there was new US legislation which limited the levels of noxious gases in vehicle exhausts (after 1968) and demanded greater attention to safety (after 1969); and on the other hand there were the massive increases in the cost of petrol which resulted first from the Arab-Israeli War in 1973, and then from the Iranian Revolution in 1979.

The confusion these changes caused was most apparent in the products of the US domestic manufacturers. Limiting exhaust emissions was most easily achieved by adding various devices to the engine, most of which decreased performance at the same time as increasing fuel consumption. Adding safety-features tended to make cars heavier, and so further limit performance and increase consumption. Thus, when the US Government drew up more new legislation to control fuel economy in the mid-1970s, the US manufacturers suddenly found themselves forced to downsize both cars and engines drastically. The results were not always happy, particularly in the sportscar market.

Meanwhile, the European manufacturers remained as keen as ever to sell sportscars in the US, and adapted their existing models to meet the new legislation. Thus older models still in production at the beginning of the decade sprouted ugly impact-resistant bumpers in their US-market versions, although for the most part they retained their original lines in other markets. Emissions control gear on US-market models so damaged performance that it was left off similar cars for other markets, with the inevitable result that the cost of producing two widely different versions of the same car had to be passed on to the customers.

As for new models, these had to be developed to meet anticipated US legislation as well as that already in force. The widespread (but mistaken) belief that open cars would be banned on safety grounds discouraged manufacturers worldwide from developing such models. In Britain, Triumph's 1970 Stag grand tourer compromised by having a roll-over bar; its 1975 TR7 was (initially at least) strictly a fixed-head coupe; and Jaguar's 1975 XJ-S was also conceived as a grand touring coupe rather than a proper sportscar. In Japan, the Datsun 240Z (which actually appeared in 1969) was designed as a closed coupe, while the Italians gave the 1972 Fiat X1/9 a Targa-type roof with a strong roll-over bar at the rear. Even the American manufacturers shied away from open cars, and the last open Corvette was made in 1975. Not until the end of the decade did open cars reappear, among the first being Triumph's reworked TR7. It was typical of the problems afflicting the British manufacturers at this stage that the car was ready for introduction in 1978 but did not actually appear until 1980.

PREVIOUS PAGE: Datsun's 1969 240Z was the first really significant Japanese sportscar and became a best-seller. It had a 2.4-liter six-cylinder engine.

LEFT: Mercedes-Benz pursued their quest for refinement in the sportscar with 1971's SLC coupe, here in 350SLC guise with 3.5-liter V8 power.

ABOVE: Jaguar put their new 5.3-liter V12 engine into the E-type in 1971, but the gains were in refinement rather than in performance.

RIGHT: Triumph's Stag grand tourer was another refined sporting model, although problems with its 3-liter V8 engine led to poor sales and an early demise.

Cars like the mid-engined Fiat and the rear-engined 1969 VW/Porsche 914 showed in the early years of the decade that the traditional British roadsters from MG and Triumph had rested on their laurels for too long and were now hopelessly outmoded. Worse still, British cars went through a period of poor build quality in the 1970s, which allowed the reliable and well-made German cars and the Datsun to increase their grip on the market.

Sales of popular sportscars took a further knock when Volkswagen introduced its 1976 Golf GTI, a socially responsible small family sedan with sportscar performance and handling, and the edges of the sportscar market in Europe were blurred by cars like the 1969 Ford Capri. The Capri was essentially a two-door sedan with a fastback body, and in base-model 1300 form it was certainly not a sportscar. Further up the range, however, the bigger-engined models did offer sportscar performance and handling, and there was no doubt that the Capri and its rivals attracted many customers who in former times would have chosen a more traditional sportscar.

Front-engine, rear-drive cars were still in the majority, and the Fiat X1/9 was alone in bringing the mid-engined layout to the popular sportscar market. Mid-engined cars still stayed mostly at the very top of the market, examples being Maserati's 1971 Bora, Ferrari's Berlinetta Boxer, Lamborghini's Countach from 1973, and BMW's M1 from 1979. There was little excitement elsewhere, either, although Mazda's rotary-engined RX-7 of 1978 was a brave (and successful) attempt by a Japanese manufacturer to bring some color to the sportscar scene. In fact, there were few engineering advances in the sportscars of the 1970s which had not been prompted by the new challenges of the era. Although fuel injection did become more widespread, it was mainly employed as a way of meeting exhaust emissions requirements, and the interest in turbocharging was mainly because it offered a chance to improve performance without harming fuel economy.

Nevertheless, both performance and handling did improve during the 1970s, the latter helped to some extent by the availability of new low-profile tires. Fuel injection and turbocharging both offered the possibility of faster acceleration as well as better fuel economy, and Porsche made use of the latter in its 1975 911 Turbo while Jaguar turned to fuel injection for its XJ-S. By the end of the decade, most of the Italian supercars were capable of 160mph, although the top speed of the popular sports models had not increased by much and was still generally around 110mph.

The most memorable sportscars of the decade were the Fiat X1/9, the Datsun 240Z, the Porsche 924 and the Lamborghini Countach. The Fiat scored for its technical bravery in a market dominated by conservative designs; and the Datsun was not only Japan's first serious sportscar export but also became the best-selling sportscar of all time. The Porsche, introduced in 1976, was the German company's first front-engined design and broadened its market base; and the Lamborghini was memorable for its sensational styling and the 190mph top speed which it could acheive with its mid-mounted transverse V12 engine.

From Musclecar to Crisis 207

LEFT: Ferrari's first stunner of the decade was the 1973 365 GT4 BB, or Berlinetta Boxer. It had a 380bhp 4.4-liter quad-cam flat-12 mounted amidships, and could exceed 160mph.

ABOVE: Fiat also used a mid-mounted engine – a more modest 1290cc four-cylinder – in their 1972 X1/9 model. Handling was a strength, but the performance was less impressive.

BELOW: Also mid-engined, and the result of collaboration between the two manufacturers, was the Volkswagen-Porsche 914. However, it lacked a clear identity and never sold as well as its makers had hoped.

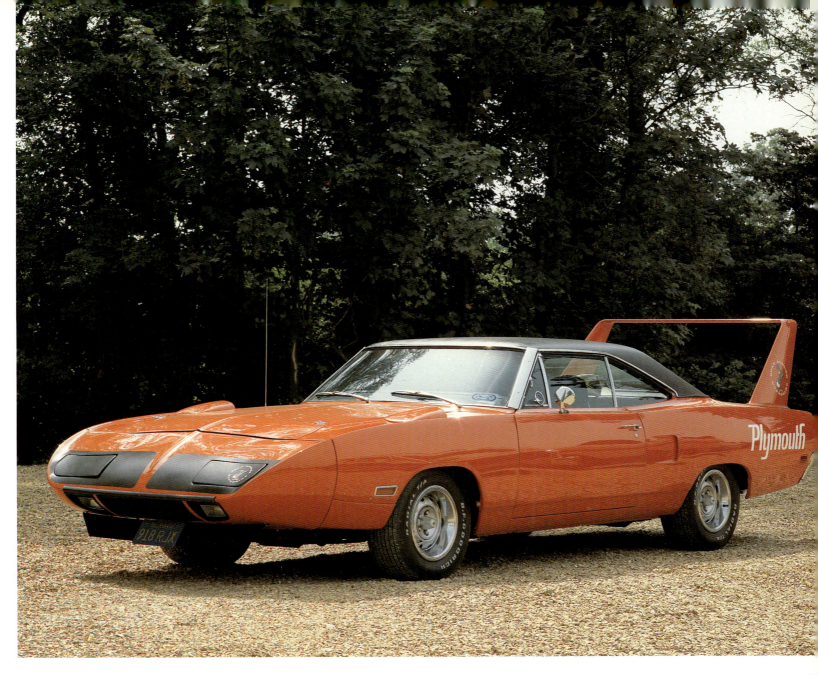

The last fling of the big-engined American sportscar was in the early 1970s. Top left is a 1970 Boss 429 Ford Mustang, with a 7-liter V8 engine; above is an outrageously-styled Plymouth Roadrunner Superbird from the same year, with a 7.2-liter V8; and left and right are examples of the evergreen Chevrolet Corvette. The 1975 roadster on the left was to be the last open Corvette for more than a decade because its makers believed safety legislation in the US would outlaw open cars.

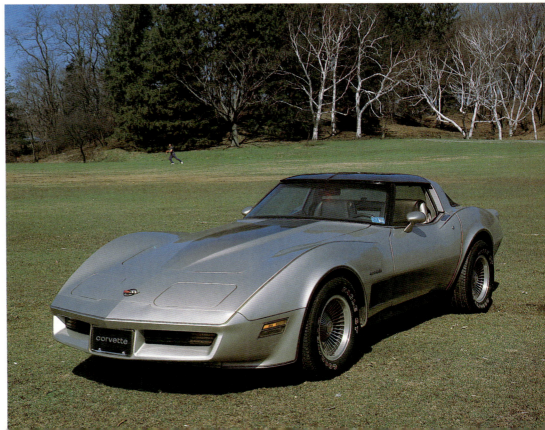

210 The Sportscar Album

LEFT: The Alfa Romeo Montreal of 1970 was a 135mph two-seater coupe with Bertone styling and a quad-cam, race-bred V8 engine. Sales were small, however.

BELOW: Built between 1967 and 1972, the Matra 530 was a rather awkwardly-styled, French-made 2+2 coupe with a 1.7-liter German Ford V4 engine.

RIGHT: The Iso Grifo married Italian styling to American power trains. This 1971 Mk II model had a 5.7-liter Chevrolet V8 engine.

BELOW RIGHT: The styling of the 1971 Marcos Mantis was definitely an acquired tatse. Production stopped after 32 examples of these Triumph 2½-liter-engined cars had been built.

LEFT: The Maserati Indy was a Vignale-styled four-seater with 155mph-plus performance from a quad-cam V8. It was built between 1969 and 1974.

RIGHT: Bertone styled the Lamborghini Espada 4000GT, another four-seat supercar of the early 1970s. Its quad-cam V12 gave 155mph performance.

BELOW: Alfa Romeo's gorgeous Spyder started life in 1966 as the Duetto and remained available in the early 1990s. This is a 1972 1750 model, with twin-cam 1779cc engine and sawn-off tail on the Pininfarina body.

From Musclecar to Crisis 213

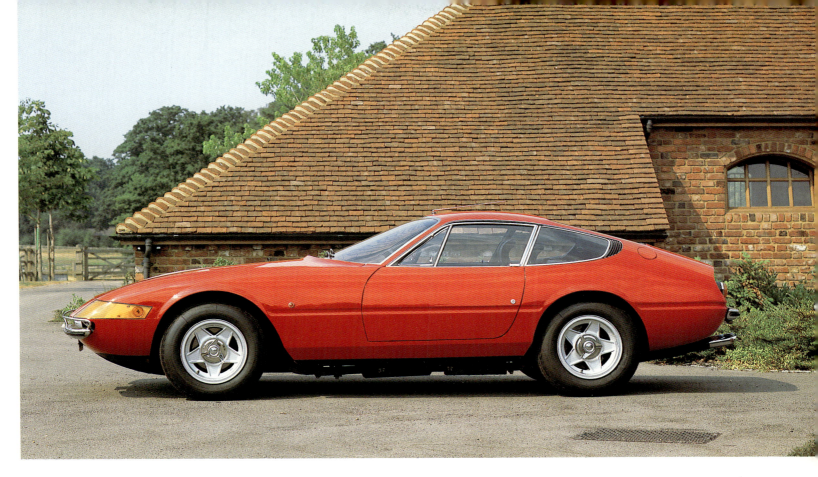

The Ferrari model-ranges of the 1970s were as complicated as ever. The small-engined model of the early 1970s was the Dino 246GT (TOP LEFT). Its rear-mounted quad-cam 2½-liter V6 engine gave 195bhp and a 150mph top speed. The traditional Ferrari with large front-mounted V12 was represented by the Daytona, usually seen as a 365GTB4 coupe (above), but also available between 1970 and 1973 as a stunning 365GTS4 convertible (LEFT). Just 121 of these were built.

During the 1970s, BMW and Porsche reigned supreme as the makers of German sporting machinery. The big BMW 3.0 CSL coupe (LEFT) was good for 137mph. Porsche's rear-engined 911 appeared in several different guises, those shown here being the 165bhp 911 Targa (ABOVE RIGHT), the 260bhp Turbo (ABOVE, FAR RIGHT) and the 300bhp racing lightweight Carrera RSR (BELOW). The front-engined 924 of 1975 (BELOW RIGHT) was an entry-level model, originally developed for Audi.

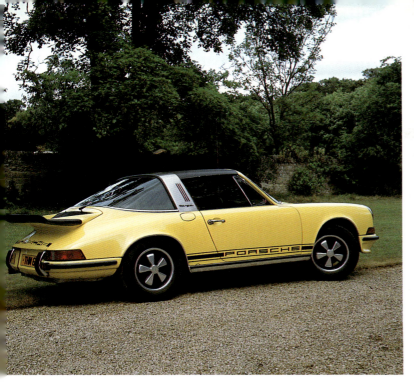

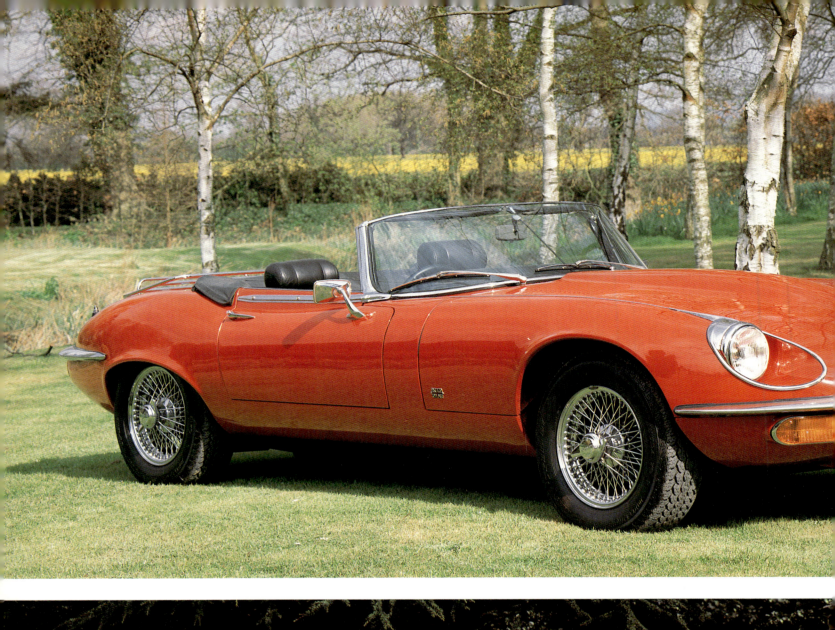

The old-style British sportscar was represented in the early 1970s by the Triumph TR6 (ABOVE), which was good for 120mph with its fuel-injected 2½-liter six, and by the Lotus Elan Sprint (BELOW LEFT), last and fastest of a range introduced in 1962. But times were changing: Jaguar had introduced a big V12 engine to refine their E-type (ABOVE LEFT), and 1970's new model from Triumph was the refined Stag grand tourer (BELOW) with its characteristic T-shaped rollover bar.

More Britons: top left is the MGB V8, with a Rover 3½-liter power unit giving 125mph. Above is the Lotus Europa Twin-cam with mid-engine. Left is a 1975 Jensen-Healey, and below is a 1973 AC 428 convertible with Frua body and 345bhp V8. Top right is the high-performance Vantage version of Aston Martin's V8 coupe. Jaguar's XJ-S grand tourer, no real replacement for the E-type, is shown below right.

222 The Sportscar Album

The success of the Japanese Datsun 240Z (TOP LEFT) made other manufacturers sit up and take notice. BMW's M1 supercar (ABOVE) and Lancia's Stratos (RIGHT) were limited-production high-performance models. In France, Renault continued to supply engines for the Alpine coupes, a four-cylinder for the A110 (LEFT) and a 2.7-liter V6 by the time of the 1979 A310 (BELOW).

From Musclecar to Crisis 223

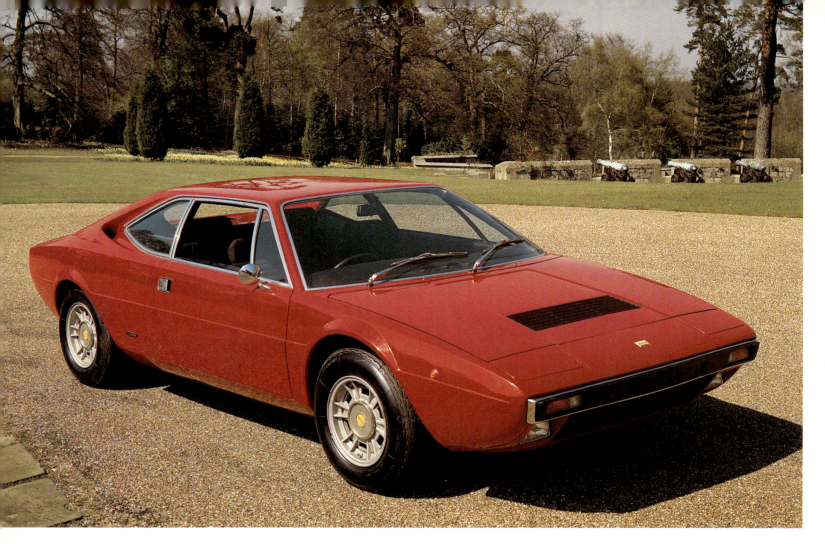

Italy remained the style leader in the 1970s. The Ferrari Dino 308GT4 (ABOVE) and 308GTB (ABOVE RIGHT) shared the same 3-liter V8 engine, but had totally different styling by Bertone and Pininfarina respectively. Pininfarina also styled the lovely four-seater Ferrari (RIGHT), which by 1977 had become a 400 with automatic transmission. The Maserati Khamsin (LEFT) had a 4.9-liter quad-cam V8.

From Musclecar to Crisis 227

Real open cars largely disappeared in the later 1970s, although Alfa Romeo continued to make their Spyder, now a Veloce and with 2-liter engine (LEFT). The Lancia Beta 2000 (BELOW LEFT) came as a coupe or as a cautious Targa-topped model, and Ford in America took much the same approach with variants of their Mustang: shown below is a 1978 T-roof King Cobra model. A big American Ford V8 powered the Italian De Tomaso Pantera coupe (RIGHT).

Chapter SEVEN

The Challenge from the East

The 1970s all but destroyed the traditional sportscar market. By the end of the decade, the British manufacturers had given up: the MG Midget, MGB and Triumph Spitfire all ceased production in 1980, and the Triumph TR7 (now in more promising open form) and its bigger-engined US-market only TR8 cousin were dropped in 1981. Jaguar no longer made a true sportscar, for the XJ-S had developed into a large and luxurious grand tourer, and Lotus, though still building sportscars, had gone up-market. The evergreen Alfa Romeo Spyder and Fiat 124 from Italy soldiered on, but as glorious anachronisms. The American manufacturers were still in disarray, and the latest Corvettes, Camaros and Mustangs offered little new to tempt buyers. Not until 1986 did an open Corvette become available once again.

Into this vacuum stepped the Japanese manufacturers. As had always been the Japanese way, their sportscars were essentially conservative, drawing on technology which had been developed but not exploited by the European makers during the 1970s. For the first half of the 1980s, Japanese sportscars were mainly coupes, laden with recent technology in the shape of multi-valve engines, computer-controlled fuel injection, anti-lock brakes, turbochargers and the like. Typical was the 1982 Mitsubishi Starion Turbo, a big coupe which offered nothing radically new, but it combined existing technology into an attractive package.

In the face of Japanese build quality and value-for-money pricing, the European manufacturers found it hard to fight back. They were unable, for example, to follow up Audi's revolutionary four-wheel-drive Quattro sports coupe, which became a model for works rally cars rather than a model for the sportscar market. They were unable, or unwilling, to follow up Fiat's now ageing X1/9, and it was Toyota who did so with the 1984 MR2. It was the Japanese Mazda company, and not a British manufacturer, which revived the traditional roadster with 1988's MX-5 Miata, and its makers openly acknowledged their debt to the MGB and the original Lotus Elan of the 1960s. Only Mercedes-Benz, always somewhat aloof from the rest of the market, came up with a real stunner in the shape of its new SL models in 1989. These brilliantly combined high safety levels (including a self-erecting roll-over bar) with high performance and the latest engine technology – but

The Challenge from the East 231

PREVIOUS PAGE: Japanese sportscars came to dominate the 1980s and 1990s. This is a 1990 Nissan 200SX, with 171bhp turbocharged 16-valve 1.8-liter engine.

LEFT: Also turbocharged was the Mitsubishi Starion 2000, which proved successful in competition.

ABOVE: Audi's revolutionary four-wheel-drive Quattro of 1980 inspired many imitators. It had a turbocharged 2.2-liter five-cylinder engine.

RIGHT: Mercedes-Benz continued to view refinement and safety as essential ingredients in the sportscar. The 1989 500SL had these in abundance, and would have exceeded 155mph comfortably but for a speed limiting device fitted as standard.

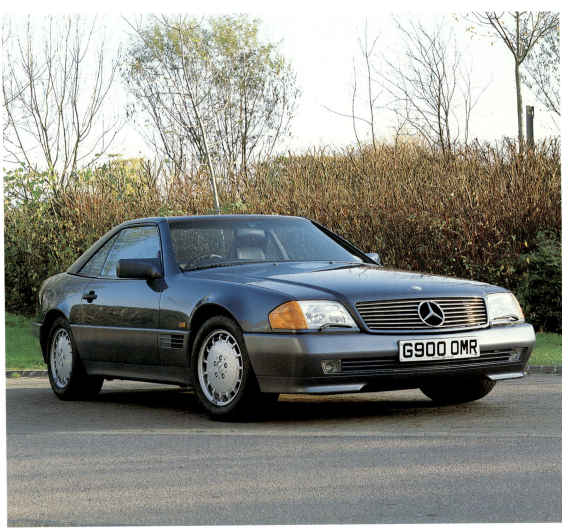

their high cost put them beyond the reach of all but the very wealthy.

There were brave tries further down the market, of course. Reliant developed a new roadster for the popular market which it called the S.S.1, using bought-in engines and a plastic body, but quality problems and inadequate performance hindered its success. Also in Britain, Lotus developed a new Elan for the roadster market (using Japanese engines), but its acknowledged excellence was never matched by profitability, and it only lasted from 1989 until 1992. In Germany, BMW experimented with the Z1, a high-performance roadster pitched rather too high up the market to have a lasting impact, although the company had no difficulty in selling those it made. Lastly, Ford exploited its links with Mazda to develop a new budget-priced roadster which it launched in 1989 as the Capri in Australia and the Mercury XR2 in the US; but sales proved disappointing.

The later 1980s saw an economic boom in the West, and sportscar makers at the top of the market exploited it ruthlessly by means of hugely expensive limited editions. Aston Martin in Britain produced the 180mph Vantage Zagato in 1988: Porsche in Germany came up with the 197mph 959 in 1987; and Ferrari made small numbers of its 190mph 288GTO (1986) and its "40th Anniversary" 201mph F40 (1987). Their success persuaded other manufacturers to follow suit. Within three years, Jaguar had announced its XJ 220; racing car manufacturer McLaren had developed an exclusive roadgoing model; a business consortium had revived the Bugatti name for another new supercar; and a second consortium had come up with the astonishing Cizeta-Moroder V16.

As far as the mainstream sportscar market was concerned, however, these 200mph supercars were largely irrelevant; and all the more so because the recession which struck Western economies in the early 1990s hit the car market very hard. It remains to be seen whether sales in the rest of the decade will match the optimism which prompted the Rover Group in Britain to reintroduce a much-modified MGB (the MG RV8) in 1992 and Chrysler in the US to announce the brutally powerful 400bhp V10-engined Dodge Viper.

ABOVE: Brute power returned to the American sportscar in 1992 with the V10-engined Dodge Viper, which also had remarkably good looks.

LEFT: Re-engined and restyled, the MGB returned in 1992 as the RV8. Its engine was a 190bhp 3.9-liter V8 which gave a 135mph top speed.

RIGHT: For the very wealthy, the 1991 Bugatti EB110 revived a famous name. Its rear-mounted 3½-liter V12 engine gave 550bhp and 211mph.

The Challenge from the East 233

234 The Sportscar Album

The Challenge from the East 235

Stylish sportscars did not have to be expensive in the 1980s: the Marcos, first seen in 1963, could be built up at home (ABOVE LEFT). It did not look out of place in the company of high-priced Italian exotica like the Targa-topped Ferrari 308GTS (ABOVE, FAR LEFT), the Lamborghini Countach (ABOVE), or the Ferrari 288GTO (BELOW). The Countach had arresting styling and enormous performance; the 288GTO was a 400bhp limited-edition model built in the mid-1980s.

Maserati was producing more practical sportscars by the late 1980s, of which the Biturbo Spyder (MAIN PICTURE) was typical. Exotica of the period included the 163mph Isdera Spyder (TOP FAR LEFT), built in Germany with a Mercedes-Benz engine mounted amidships, and the 1989 Ferrari 348 (ABOVE LEFT), the first roadgoing Ferrari to have a monocoque body instead of a tubular chassis. In the early 1990s a new more brutal styling trend emerged in cars such as the Zagato-bodied Alfa Romeo SZ coupe (ABOVE RIGHT).

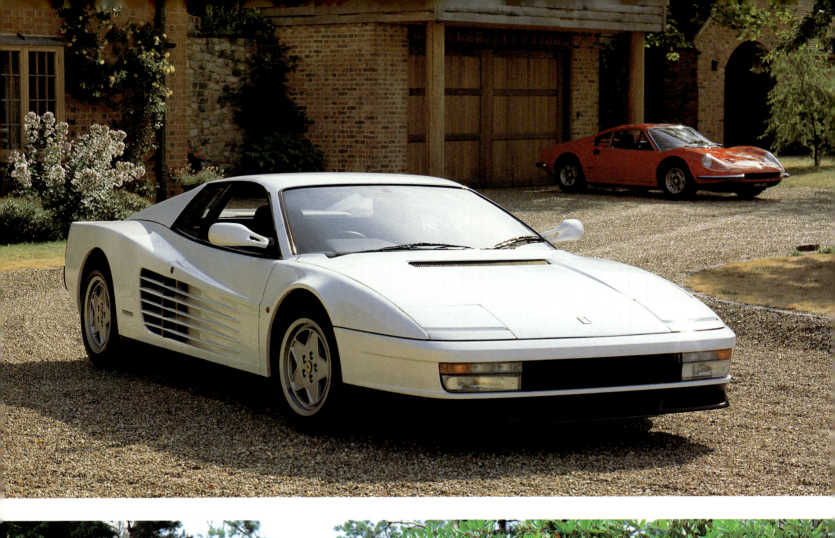

The Challenge from the East 239

Italian supercars for the 1990s: on the left is the Ferrari Testarossa, introduced in 1984 with flat-12 engine and re-engineered for 1992 as the 512TR (BELOW). To celebrate 40 years in the car-making business in 1987, Ferrari introduced the F40 (BELOW LEFT), a limited-edition model with a turbocharged 32-valve 3-liter V8 which gave over 200mph. The Bugatti EB110 (CENTER RIGHT) was designed by the former Ferrari engineer responsible for the F40, and had a 60-valve V12 engine with four turbochargers. Lamborghini's astonishing Diablo (TOP RIGHT) was the fastest-ever road car when it was launched in 1990, but its 201mph top speed has since been bettered by several rivals.

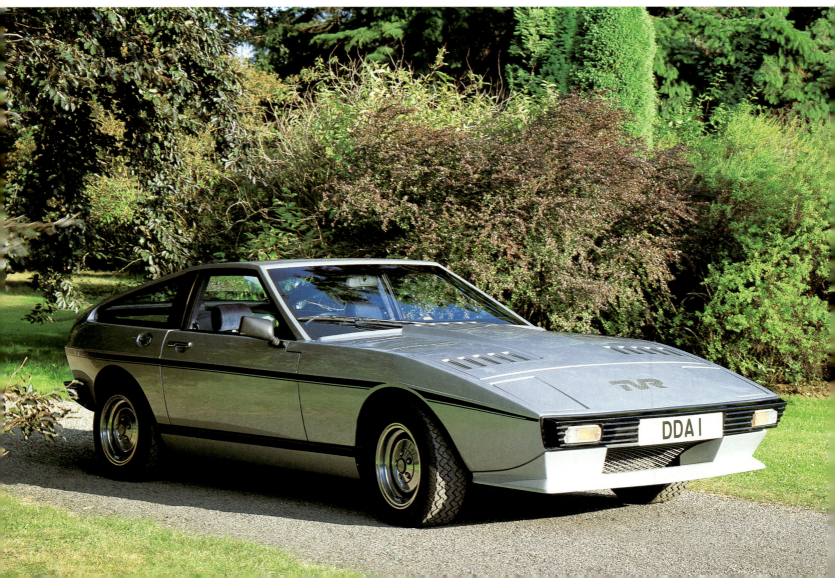

The Challenge from the East 241

The high-performance British sportscar of the 1980s and 1990s was still represented by Aston Martin, whose experimental Bulldog (LEFT) did not enter production, but whose big Vantage V8 (CENTER RIGHT) sold strongly to wealthy clients. TVR had meanwhile graduated to a much more refined range of models; the 1980 V6-powered Taimar (TOP RIGHT) harked back to earlier models, but the 1981 Tasmin (BELOW LEFT) was of the new school. Small manufacturer Ginetta came up with the G33 (BELOW) in 1990, which did 145mph on its 3.9-liter V8 engine. Financial problems overcame the DeLorean (FAR LEFT), but not before large numbers of this V6-engined coupe had been made.

As the 1980s ended, convertibles began to return. Typical were the open Jaguar XJ-S (LEFT), the limited-edition Aston Martin Volante Zagato (BELOW), and the ill-fated Lotus Elan SE (BOTTOM LEFT), which was withdrawn in 1992 when a market slump hit its makers. Big coupes still mattered, though: Aston Martin introduced their new 160mph Virage (RIGHT) in 1988, and Jaguar announced the limited-edition XJ220 sports-racer, of which a 1988 prototype is pictured (ABOVE, FAR LEFT).

LEFT: TVR's 350i was a mid-1980s model which mated Rover V8 power to the wedge-shaped body pioneered by the Tasmin.

BELOW LEFT: Reliant's brave attempt to build an affordable sportscar in the mid-1980s was not initially a success; but a facelift and a turbocharged Nissan engine made it into the vastly improved Scimitar SST Turbo.

RIGHT: BMW's striking Z1 2½-liter roadster was far too expensive to succeed in the small sportscar market, but as a limited edition it was a success.

BELOW: Renault's GTA Turbo was a V6-powered coupe in the Alpine sportscar tradition, and it spearheaded the French company's quest for a revitalized image in the late 1980s.

Porsche offered a wide variety of models in the 1980s and 1990s. The 944S (LEFT), was based loosely on the entry-level 924 but offered much greater performance. The 928 (RIGHT) was first seen in the 1970s and had Porsche's first production V8 engine; by the time of the 1988 S4 version pictured here, it had become a high-performance luxury coupe. The 911 remained hugely popular, despite its age, and a 1986 Carrera is pictured (BELOW LEFT). The 959 (BELOW RIGHT) was a competition derivative of the 911, with a 400bhp racing engine, and was produced in only limited numbers.

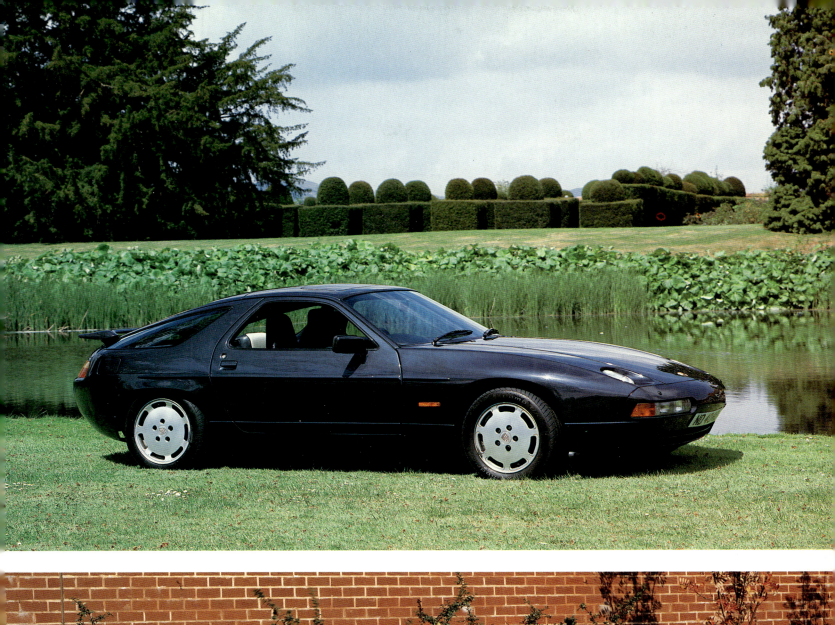

The Challenge from the East 249

TOP LEFT: Convertibles returned to America slowly in the 1980s, and the Ford Mustang of 1983 was among the first. Pictured is a 1986 5-liter GT version.

BOTTOM LEFT: More powerful engines gradually returned in the later 1980s. The top performance package for 1989 Chevrolet Camaro IROC-Z models, like this one, was a 240bhp, 5.7-liter V8.

ABOVE: The Pontiac Firebird resolutely retained its fixed roof. The base-model had a V6 engine, but all other versions had V8s by the time this 1987 example was built.

RIGHT: German manufacturers, especially BMW, had turned to the high-performance sedan during the 1980s. This is a BMW M3 Sport Evolution of 1990, based on the small 3-series sedan but offering performance of a completely different order.

ABOVE: The sixth-generation Chevrolet Corvette arrived in 1984. This 1987 model, with a 240bhp V8 engine, shows off its finely-chiselled lines.

LEFT: Top performance option for the Corvette was the ZR-1, with a Lotus-developed 375bhp V8 which gave shattering acceleration and a 180mph top speed.

ABOVE RIGHT: The sportscar gone soft: Datsun's 280ZX was too much of a boulevard cruiser and was a disappointment after the earlier 240Z and 260Z models.

RIGHT: Mazda's RX-7 had a delightfully smooth and responsive Wankel rotary engine, and showed that Japanese makers were a force to be reckoned with. The car lasted from 1978 until 1991.

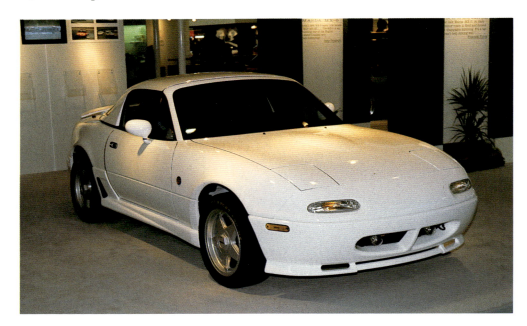

Japanese manufacturers dominated the sportscar scene of the 1980s and 1990s. Top left is Mazda's 1988 MX-5 roadster, seen here with optional hardtop. Left is the mid-engined Toyota MR-2, another "affordable" sportscar introduced in 1984. Below, the second-generation Mazda RX-7 could be had as a convertible. Honda's second-generation CRX with electrically retractable roof center section (BELOW FAR RIGHT) offered speeds up to 130mph from just 1.6 liters, while the V6 3-liter Honda NSX (BELOW RIGHT), which entered production in 1990, was a 165mph challenger to the Italian supercars. Nissan's 1989 300ZX (RIGHT) redeemed the company from its 280ZX mistake, offering 155mph performance in a svelte body.

The wave of new aerodynamic shapes and the advent of safety and emissions legislation created a market both for classic cars and for "retro-classics" – cars which looked as if they belonged to the uncomplicated days of old but were actually equipped to modern standards. One of the successful early entrants to this market was Panther, whose 1972 Jaguar-engined J72 (LEFT) was styled to resemble the SS 100 sportscar of the 1930s. More recently, the big Austin-Healey of the 1950s and 1960s has been revived, now with Rover V8 power and bearing the name of the Healey 3500 Mk IV (BELOW).

Index

Page numbers in *italics* refer to illustrations.

Abarth 1950s 747cc coupe *155*
ABC 1924 SuperSports *51*
AC 84
  1933 16/60 2-liter six *94*
  1936 16/80 2-liter six 44, *115*
  1954 Ace 2-liter six *159*, 182
  1955 Aceca fixed-head coupe *162*
  1964/6 Cobra, Le Mans and Mark III *183*
  1970s 428 convertible *220*
Alfa Romeo 42, 80, 82, 137, 172
  1922 RL racing version *42*
  1920s 22/90 2994cc six *42*
  1927 1500cc tourer *42*
  1929 1750 six 42, *73*, 82, *86*
  1931 8C-2300 Le Mans car 82, *86-7*
  1934 six cylinder 82
  1936 2.9-liter model *80*, 134
  1955 Giulietta Sprint 137, *156*
  1950s SZ coupe 137, *237*
  1963 TZ sports racer *157*
  1966 Duetto 170, 212
  1970 Montreal coupe *210*
  1972 1750 Spyder *212*, 230
    Veloce 2-liter *226*
Allard, Sidney 143
  1946 K1 V8 134, *143*
  1952 J2X sports racer *149*
Alvis 40, 82
  1922 12/40 Sports Model *41*
  1923 12/50 "Duck's Back" *41*, *49*
  1920s 1.5-liter *38*
  1932 Speed Twenty 2.5-liter *101*
  1930s Speed Twenty Five *128*
  1966 TF21 sports sedan *185*
Amilcar 45, 63, 70
  1921 CS voiturette 44, *52*
  1923 CGS Grand Sports 44, *52*
    CGSS "Surbaisse" 53, *68*
  1925, 1926 versions 44-5
Armstrong-Siddeley,
  5-liter Siddeley Special 92
  1929 Apline Trial tourer *92*
Aston Martin 51, 84, 173
  1924 sports racer *51*, 84
  1926 1.5-liter International *59*
  1934 1.5-liter Mark II *98*
  1936 2-liter Le Mans *99*
  1930s Ulster *100*
  1940s DB1 *142*
  1950 DB2 138
  1958 DB4 3.6-liter 138, *138*
  1960 DB4GT sports racer *179*
  1964-5 DB5 *182*
    DB6 *187*
  1969 DBS 5.3-liter V8 *186*, *221*
  1988 Vantage Zagato 232, *241*, *243*
  1988 Virage *243*
  1980s Bulldog *240*
Auburn 16, 75
  1928 4.5-liter Speedster *43*, 84
  1930s Speedster 85, *85*
Audi Quattro sports coupe 230, *231*
Austin,
  1920s Seven 45, 61, *61*

1929/30 Ulster 45, *63*, *90*
Austin Healey 137
  1955 100S 4-cylinder *159*
  1950s 100/6 sportscar *147*
  1958 BN4 2+2 model *164*
  1958 "frogeye" 948cc four *165*
  1959 3000 model *176*
  1970s/80s 3500 Mark IV *254*
Austro Daimler,
  1910 27/80 Prince Henry 12, 72
  1927 3-liter 19/100 *72-3*
Auto Union GP cars 80

Ballot 1922/3 cars 54, *54*
Bamford and Martin company 51
Barker, bodywork by *39*
Bentley 68, 82, 85, 89, 118
  1920s 3-liter 38, 41
  1926 3-liter Speed model *39*
  1927 4.5-liter four 41
  1928 "Blue Train" *111*
  1929 Speed Six 41
  1930 8-liter 41
  "Blower" *77-8*
Benz 38
  1908 GP four *22-3*
  1911-14 cars 12
  1919 sports tourer *32*
Bertelli, A C bodywork by *59*, *88*
Bertone styling *156*, *192-3*, *210*, *213*, *224*
Besley, P F *58*
Biddle 1918 Model K roadster *34*
Bignan 1924 2-liter car 44
Birkigt, Marc 15, 40
Bleriot Whippet cyclecar *53*
BMW 85, 216
  328 sports model *83*, 85, *125*
  1956 507 3168cc V8 *156*
  1979 M1 206, *222*
  1970s CSL 3.0 coupe 216
  1980s Z1 roadster 232, *245*
  1990 M3 Sports Evolution *249*
Bond 1969 Equipe 2-liter six *189*
Borbeau and Devaux cyclecar 15
Brasier racing car 21
Bristol 125, 134
  1950s 400 sports sedan *142*
  1954 404 coupe *162*
British Motor Industry Heritage Trust Collection, Gaydon 45
Brough Superior 114
  1935 sports tourer *115*
  1936 Alpine Grand Sport 114
    four-door sedan 114
  1937 drophead coupe *120*
BSA,
  1929-36 three-wheeler *91*
  1935 Scout *128*, 129
Bugatti, Ettore 10,12, 40
Bugatti cars 80, 82, 232
  1911 1460 cc ohc 12
  1920 Type T23 Brescia 40
  1925 model *70*
  1924-30 Type 35 40, 42
  1926 Type 35B *40*
  1927 Type 43 *72*
  1929 Type 46 113
  1935 Type 57T *88*
  1930s Atalanta *88-9*
  1937 Type 57SC *118*
  1939 T 57SC Corsica *127*
  1991 EB110 232, *233*, *239*

Calthorpe 1908 model *25*
Canstatt-Daimler 1899 car 8, 10
Carrington coachwork *121*
Chrysler Dodge Viper 232, *232*
Cisitalia cars 134
Citroën 53
  1934 Ranelagh tourer *111*
Cizeta-Moroder V16 232
Clyno 1923 10.8hp Sports *48*
Cord, E L 43
Cord cars 16, 42-3, 85, 111
  1928 Model J 42-3

1935 V8 85
1930s Model 810 Lycoming *131*
Cottin-Desgouttes 1925 3-liter *68-9*
Crossley 12
  1912 15hp Shelsley 13, *13*
Crouch 1913 model *30*
cyclecars 15, 41, *53*, *91*

Daimler, Paul 10
Daimler, Coventry,
  c1904 4-cylinder chain drive 10
  1930s Double-Six *110*
  1959 SP250 V8 *177*
Darracq company 127
Datsun,
  1969 240Z coupe *202-3*, 204, 206, 222, 250
  1980s 280Z *251*
De Dietrich 10, 29
  1903 45hp model 10, 21
  1905 12-liter 670, 10, *11*
    24hp model *21*
De Dion-Bouton 1909 1.8-liter *26*
De Tomaso,
  1963 Vallelunga *192*
  1970s Pantera coupe *227*
Delage 12, 82, 89, 117, 127
  1911 3-liter 12
  1913 DI *31*
  1921 14/40 tourer 44
  1924 DI tourer *55*
  1929 6-cylinder tourer *70*
  1937 D8 4.3-liter *81*
  1939 D6-75 *127*
Delahaye 89, 111, 127
  1936 3.2-liter Coupe des Alpes 117
  1936 3.5-liter Type 135 *117*
  1937 3.5-liter Le Mans *120*
  1937 4.5-liter Type 165 *122*
  1952 Type 235 *148*
DeLorean V6 coupe *240*
Don, Kaye 63
Douglas 1921 1.2-liter *47*
Duesenberg 42, 85, 111
  1921 Model A tourer 42, *43*
  1928 Model J *66-7*, *106*, 107
  1929 model *84*
Duntov, Zora Arkus 151
Dupont 1929 Model G Speedster *66*

Edge, S F 10
Edwards, T. L. 57
EHP 1925 voiturette *58*
ERA racing cars 97
Essex 1919 2.9-liter four *46*

Facel Vega 1954 V8 coupe 138
Ferrari, Enzo 42, 137
Ferrari 137, 173
  1945 250GT coupe 138
  1949 166 2-liter V12 *132-3*, 137
  1956 250GT *153*
  1960 250GT Berlinetta *191*
  1962 250GTO *190*
  1965 275GTB *194*, 195
  1967 330GTC *195*
  1968 365GTB Daytona *195*, *215*
  1960s 275GTB4 *172-3*
  1973 365GT4 Berlinetta Boxer 206, *206*
  1977 400 four-seater *225*
  1970s 246GT Dino *214*
    308GT4 Dino *224*
    308GTB *225*
    365GTS4 convertible *214-15*
  1984 Testarossa *238*
  1986 288GTO 232, *234-5*
  1987 F40 "40th Anniversary" 232, *238*
  1989 348 *239*
  1980s 308GTS Targa-Top *234*
  1992 512TR *239*
Fiat 10, 54, 172
  1927 Tipo 520, 521 77
  1928 Tipo 525 *76*
  1932 Tipo 508 Balilla *90*

1965 850 Spyder *193*
1966 124 Spyder 170, 230
1972 X1/9 204, 207, *207*, 230
Ford,
  1922 Model T Speedster *58*
  1955 Thunderbird 138, *151*
  1960s GT40 V8 *198*
  1964 Mustang *172-3*, 197, 199, 230
    1966 Convertible *2-3*
    1966 4.7-liter V8 *197*
    1969 "Mach 1" *200*
    1970 Boss 429 *208*
    1978 T-roof King Cobra *227*
    1986 5-liter GT *248*
  1969 Capri 1300 *206*
  1989 Capri (Mercury XR2) *232*
Francois, Jean, design by *122*
Frazer-Nash, Archie 16
Frazer Nash 16, 84, 120, 134
  1.5-liter sports tourer *65*
Frau styling *193*, *220*

General Motors 38, 137
  1954 Chevrolet Corvette *136*, *137-8*
  1956 *150*
  1958-62 *155*, 173, *175*
  1960s Sting Ray model *171*, *199*
  1968 *201*, 204, *208-9*, 230
  1984-7 ZR1 230, *250*
  1966-7 Chevrolet Camaro 173, *199*, 230
  1989 Chevrolet Camaro IROC-Z *248*
Ghia coachwork *192*
Gilbern 1960s Genie V6 *189*
Giles, Eric, design by *88*
Ginetta 1990 G33 V8 *241*
GN 65, 120
  cyclecar 16, *17*
    GP version 16, *17*
  1920 Vitesse 1.1-liter *46*
Godfrey, H R 16, 20
Gordon Bennett Trophy 19, 21, 32
Grand Prix races 12, 42, *42*, 72
Grand Prix de Tourisme *53*
grande routière cars 82, 134, 138
Gregoire, J A 65
  1929 Tracta 1.5-liter *64*

Hawthorn, Mike 97
HE cars,
  1920 14/20 tourer *59*
  1925 14/40 tourer *59*
Healey, Donald 117, 147
Healey Cars 134
  1949 Silverstone *147*, 148
  1970s/80s 3500 Mk IV *254*
Henley 1950s roadster *75*
Henry, Prince, of Prussia 15
Herkomer Trophy 10
Heynes, William 144
Hispano-Suiza,
  1912 Alfonso XIII *14*, 15
  1919 7.2-liter six 40
Honda,
  1980s/90s CRX 1.6-liter *253*
  1990 NSX *253*
Hooper coachwork *113*
Horstmann Cars Ltd 57
  Sports/Super Sports models 57
Hotchkiss 1936 686 Grand Sport *117*
HRG,
  1930s 1.5-liter model *120*, 129
  1948 1500 *140*

Invicta 82
  1927 3-liter 4-seater *36-7*
  1930 4.5-liter Sports *93*
Iso,
  1962 Rivolta GT coupe *192*
  1971 Grifo Mk II *211*
Isotta Fraschini cars *6-7*
  1906 120bhp racer 10
  1908 1200cc series 10
  1910 and 1913 models 12
Itala racers 9, *10*, *24-5*

Jaguar 84, 114, 138, 172
  1938 SS 100 3.5-liter *128*
  1948 XK120 2-seater 134, *134*
  1949 XK120 roadster *144*
  1950s XK120 138, *144-5*, 160
  1950s XK150 3.8-liter 138, *139*, 160
  1955 XK140 138, *160*
  1958 XK150S *160-61*
  1961 E-type 3.8-liter 170, 173, *180-81*, 220
  1963 E-type Series I roadster *168-9*, *180*
  1971 E-type 5.3-liter *205*, 218
  1975 XJ-S 204, 206, *221*, 230
  1980s XJ-S convertible *242*
  1990 XJ220 232, *242*
Jarrott, Charles 9, 10, 21
Jensen 1957 541R coupe *167*
Jensen-styling 100
Jensen-Healey 1975 model *220*
Jowett 1950 1486cc Jupiter *158*

Kelsch bodywork 55
Kieft 1954-6 1100 sports *152*
Kimber, Cecil 45, 102
Kissell, William and George 34
  cars by *35*, 75

Lagache-Glaszman bodywork 54
Lago, Major A F 127
Lagonda 82
  1921 11.9hp racer *47*
  1925 14/60 models *43-4*
  1931 2-liter fast tourer *92*
  1930s Rapier 82
  1937 V12 Grande *129*
Lamborghini,
  1966, Miura V12 *195*
  1970s Espada 4000GT *213*
  1970s/80s Countach 206, *235*
  1990 Diablo *239*
Lancia,
  1922 Lambda 40-41, *41*
  1931 Lambda 2.5-liter *89*
  1955 B24 V6 Spyder *151*
  1957 Aurelia GT *156*
  1965 Fulvia coupe 170
  1970s Stratos *223*
  1970s Beta 2000 *226*
Lea-Francis 84
  Hyper 1.5-liter *62*
Ledwinka, Hans 57
Lombard cars 45
Lorraine-Dietrich 29
  1910 1.6-liter DFP 29
  1912 15-liter *29*
  1913 Series M 2-seater *29*
  1924-6 3.5-liter 40
Lotus 230
  1957 Seven *164*
  1958 Elite 137, *167*
  1962 Elite Series II *178*
  1966 Europa 170, *220*
  1970s Elan Sprint *218*, 230
  1989-92 Elan SE 232, *242*

Marcos *235*
  1960 GT Ford-engined *191*
  1971 Mantis 2½-liter *211*
Marendaz 45
  1926 Special *69*
  1928 9/90 1.1-liter *44*
  1936 13/70 Special *124*
Maserati,
  1958 3500GT 138
  1964 Mistral *193*
  1969-74 Indi V8 *212*
  1971 Bora mid-engine car *206*
  1970s Khamsin 4.9-liter *224*
  1980s Biturbo Spyder *236-7*
Mathis 53, 63
  pre-WWI 1.3-liter cyclecar 53
Matra,
  1960s Djet 1-liter coupe *197*
  1967-72 530 1.7-liter coupe *210*
Mays, Raymond 97
Mazda,
  1978 RX-7 206, *251-2*
  1988 MX-5 Miata 230, *252*
McLaren roadgoing model 232
Mercedes 16, 38, 134

256 Index and Acknowledgments

1901 5.9-liter 9, 10
1903 60hp 2-seater 18
1905-6 120hp four 20
1911-12 Mercedes 90 27
c1914 117hp racing car 31
1914 7.2-liter 28/95 40
c1931 38/250 41
Mercedes-Benz 38, 41, 80, 172
  1928 38/250SS 39, 42, 75, 82
  SSK 76-7, 82
  SSKL 38, 42, 82
  38/250TT 74
  1936-9 540K 122-5
  1930s 380, 380S models 82
  1930s 500K, 540K 82
  1950s 300SL 138, 138, 152, 156
  1955-63 190SL 138, 174
  1963 230SL 170, 172, 173
  1968 250SL 173, 200
  280SL 173
  1971 350SLC coupe 204
  1989 SL models 230, 231
Mercer 16
  1911-15 Type 35 Raceabout 15, 16
Métallurgique 10-liter 100bhp 10
MG 40, 45, 84, 99, 134, 137, 172, 206
  "Old Number One" 45
  18/80, Mk II, Mk III 45
  1930s Midget 45, 68, 105
  1930s K3 Magnette 103
  1930s TA 84
  1932 Magna 102
  1932 K1 tourer 102
  1034-6 ND 1.3-liter four 103
  1936 PB 104
  1936 SA tourer 105
  1950s-60s MGA 137, 163, 166
  1960s MGB 170, 173, 188, 230
  1968 Midget 186, 230
  1970s MGB 171, 220
  1992 MG RV8 232, 232
Mitsubishi 1982 Starion Turbo 230
Morgan 137
  1913 three-wheeler 28

1928 RSS Super Sports 61
1933 Supersports 94
1936 1.1-liter 4/4 117
Morris 1928 Morris Six, Minor 45
Morris Garages 45; see MG

Napier,
  1903 30hp racer 9
  1907 Napier 60, 10, 10
  1908 R-Type 24
  1915 3-liter tourer 30
Nissan,
  1989 300ZX 253
  1990 200SX 228-9
Nuvolari, driver 54

Offord bodywork 68
Ogle 1962 SX1000 coupe 178
OM 1923 2-liter six 15/60 60
Opel cars 18-19
Osca cars 134

Packard 111
  1930s Model 734 Speedster 107
  1935-9 3.7-liter coupe 120
  1936 V12 roadster 130
Panhard 1960s 24BT 196
Panther 1972 J72 Jaguar-engined 254
Pegaso, 1950s V8 coupe 138, 154
Peugeot company 52
Pierce-Arrow 1929 convertible 67
Pininfarina styling 138, 151, 153, 156, 173, 190, 194, 212, 225
Plymouth 1970 Roadrunner Superbird V8 209
Pontiac Firebird 199, 249
Porsche, Ferdinand 12, 41
Porsche cars 170, 172, 216
  1950-65 356 models 137, 138
  1964 356 Carrera 2 175
  1960 RS60 Spyder 174
  1964-75 911 models 170, 173, 206, 216-17

1970s 914, 206, 207
1976 924 206, 216, 246
1987 959 232, 249
1980s-90s 944S 246
1986 911 Carrera 246
1988 928S4 247

Railton, Read 65
Railton cars and company 120
  1926 2-liter Arab sportscar 65
  1936-7 models 118, 121
Reliant,
  1980s SS01 roadster 232
  Scimitar, Scimitar Turbo 184, 244
Renault, Marcel 19
Renault company and cars 53, 222
  1902 3.8-liter four 18
  1980s GTA Turbo 245
Riley, Percy 41
Riley company and cars 40, 84
  1020s 11/40 Sports 41, 42
  1920s Riley Nine 68
  1920s Brooklands four 119
  1930s Imp, Lynx, Sprite 96, 97, 97, 105, 118, 119
  1950s roadster 146
Rolls Royce 12, 82
  1910 Silver Ghost 12, 26-7
  1913 Alpine Eagle 17
Rover group 232
  1930s tourer 101
  1947 12hp tourer 141
Royal Automobile Club trial 12
Rush, Harry, design by 42

Sakhnoffsky, Count Alexis de, design work by 85
Salmson 45, 63
  1929 Grand Sport 71
  1955 2300S coupe 158
Saoutchik body work 126
Scaglietti bodywork 153, 173, 190,
Scales, J E 54
S.C.A.T. 1908 racing car 22, 22
Schebera-Schapiro bodywork 26

Shelby, Carroll 199
  Mustang GT350 198
Simplex 1912 chain-drive car 32
Singer 1932 Nine Sports, Le Mans 98-9
Sizaire-Naudin voiturette 10, 11, 12
Smith and Mabley 16
  197 50bhp 9.7-liter cars 16
Squire 1930s 1.5-liter sportscar 112
S.S. cars 114; see also Jaguar
  1930s S.S.1 114
  1930s 1- and 2-liter cars 84
  1935 S.S.90 114
  1936, 1938 SS 100 82, 82, 95, 254
Standard 1929 Avon Special 100
Stanley brothers 16
  1906 Gentleman's Speedy Roadster 16
  1908 20hp model 24
Sunbeam-Talbot-Carracq (STD) 127
  1938 23CV 4-liter car 126
Steyr cars 57
Straker-Squire 12
  1918 4-liter six-cylinder 33
Studebaker company 66
Stutz, Harry C 16
Stutz cars 16
  1911-12 car 16
  1914 Bearcat 13, 15, 16, 34
  1918-20 models 34-5, 56
Sunbeam 12
  1934 Le Mans Replica 95
  1955 Alpine 146, 182, 184
  1964 Tiger 182
Swallow 1954 Doretti 163

Talbot 82, 127
  1930s 2.3 liter six 90, 108
  1931 2.9 liter sports tourer 108-9
Talbot-Lago 1949 Le Mans coupe 148
Thomas, Parry 65

Toyota 1984 MP2 230, 252
Triumph 82, 137, 172, 206
  1929 Super Seven 62
  1930s Dolomite 82, 117
  1934-5 Gloria, Gloria Vitesse 114, 114
  1936 Monte Carlo tourer 116
  1946 1800 model 141
  1953 TR2 135, 137, 138
  1961 TR4 172, 173
  1962 Spitfire 170, 185, 230
  1967 TR4A 186
  1970 Stag grand tourer 204, 205, 209
  1970s-80s TR6, TR8 219, 230
  1970s-80s TR7 204
TVR,
  1958 Grantura 176
  1967 Vixen 189
  1980 Taimar V6 241
  1981 Tasmin 240, 245
  1980s 350i 244

Van den Plas coachwork 72-3
Vauxhall 12, 38
  1910 Prince Henry 12
  1911 20hp tourer 12
  1914 Prince Henry 30/98 15, 38
  1919 E-type 30/98 38
  1922-3 models 49-50
Vernon Derby 1929 1.1-liter 63
Vignale styling 212
voiturettes 10, 16, 44, 58, 63
Volkswagen,
  Beetle 12
  1976 Golf GTi 206
Volkswagen/Porsche 914 206, 207
Volvo P1800 196
Weyman bodywork 111
Winton 1903 Bullet 32, 33
Wolseley 1933 Hornet 95, 100

Zagato bodywork 86, 137, 155, 157, 179, 237

Acknowledgments

The author and publisher would like to thank David Eldred the designer, Stephen Small the editor and picture researcher, Veronica Price and Nicki Giles for production, and Ron Watson for providing the index. The following individuals and agencies provided photographic material:

Brompton Books, pages: 9(top left), 20(both), 31(bottom), 39(bottom), 54-5, 68-9, 108(top), 123(top), 124-5, 131, 154-5, 209(bottom/Bob Baldridge)
Brompton Books/Nicky Wright, pages: 2-3, 45, 102(both), 103(bottom), 105(bottom), 135(top), 143(bottom), 196-7, 200(bottom), 208(top), 227(bottom), 248(top)
Neill Bruce, pages: 1, 10, 11(bottom), 15, 17(both), 18(top right), 18-19, 24(top & bottom right), 26(top), 36-7, 39(top), 47(bottom), 48-9, 50, 51(bottom), 54(top), 55(top), 60(top), 61(top), 62(bottom), 63(bottom), 68(top), 70(bottom), 71, 72(top), 83, 86(top), 88(top), 89(top), 90(top), 91, 92-3(all three), 94(top), 96, 98(bottom), 100(bottom), 100-1, 103(top),

107(top), 109(top), 110, 111(top), 112-3, 114(bottom), 115(bottom), 117(bottom), 120(bottom), 125(top), 128(bottom & top left), 132-3, 134, 136, 137, 140, 141(bottom), 144(bottom), 145, 148(top), 148, 153, 158(top), 159(both), 160(both), 161, 162, 164(bottom), 165, 166, 168-9, 170, 172-3, 177, 178(bottom), 179, 180(bottom), 183(bottom), 184(top), 186(bottom & top right), 187, 189(bottom), 190, 191(both), 192(bottom), 194, 195(middle), 198(top), 200(top), 202-3, 204, 206, 207(bottom), 211(bottom), 214-5(all three), 217(top right & left), 218(top), 220(top right & left), 221(bottom), 222(middle), 224(both), 225(both), 226(both), 228-9, 231(bottom), 234(top left), 234-5, 235(top), 237(top left), 238(both), 239(top & bottom), 241(middle), 242(both), 243(both), 246(bottom), 247(both), 252(top), 254(bottom)
Neill Bruce/Sven Eric Deler, pages: 174(top), 236(top)
Neill Bruce/Tobjorn Hansson, pages: 198(bottom), 199(bottom left), 248(bottom)
Neill Bruce/Midland Motor Museum, pages: 74, 82, 87(top), 109(bottom), 117(top), 116(bottom), 139(top), 144(top), 147(bottom), 152(both),

175(bottom), 178(top), 182(top), 185(bottom), 186(top left), 201, 213(top), 216(bottom), 217(bottom), 220(bottom), 221(top), 240(top left & bottom)
Neill Bruce/The Peter Roberts Collection, pages: 11(top), 21(bottom), 27(top), 28(top), 40, 43(top), 60-1, 65(top), 108(bottom), 119(top), 122(top), 128(top right), 143(top), 154(top), 164(top), 185(top), 189(top right), 196(top left), 209(top), 222-3, 227(top), 230, 232(top), 236-7, 237(top right), 241(bottom), 250(bottom), 251(both), 252(bottom), 253(all three), 254(top)
Neill Bruce/Nicky Wright, pages: 14(top), 18(top left), 66(top), 75(top), 107(top), 208(bottom), 249(top), 250(top)
Colin Burnham, pages: 150(bottom)
DH collection, pages: 14(bottom), 25(bottom), 32(bottom), 42, 107(bottom), 151(bottom), 155(top), 192(top)
Mike Key, pages: 150(top), 171(bottom), 199(top)
Lifefile/Decet, pages: 138, 167(top)
Lifefile/Guy Usher, pages: 23(top), 252(middle)
Andrew Morland, pages: 24(bottom left), 27(bottom), 30(bottom), 31(top), 35(bottom),

38, 41, 49(top), 51(top), 52(both), 58(bottom), 59(bottom), 63(top), 65(bottom), 69(top), 70(top), 73(top), 84, 86-7, 90(bottom), 94(bottom), 97(both), 98(top), 99(bottom), 101(bottom right), 111(bottom), 114(top), 115(top), 116(top), 118(both), 120(top), 121(bottom), 124(top), 130(bottom), 135(bottom), 142(both), 146(both), 147(top), 148(bottom), 156(top), 157(top), 158(bottom), 162(top), 163(both), 167(bottom), 174(bottom), 176(top), 182(bottom), 184(bottom), 188(both), 189(top left), 193(both), 195(top & bottom), 196(top right), 197(top), 199(bottom right), 205(top), 207(top), 210(bottom), 211(top), 211(top), 218(bottom), 219(both), 220(middle), 222(top right & left), 223(top), 233, 234(top right), 239(middle), 240(top right), 241(top), 244(both), 245(both), 246(top)
National Motor Museum, England, pages: 4-5, 6, 8-9, 9(top right), 13(both), 21(top), 22-3(both), 25(top), 26(bottom), 28-9, 29(top), 30(top), 32(top), 33(both), 34(both), 35(top), 43(bottom), 44, 46(bottom), 47(top), 48(top), 53(both), 56-7, 57(top), 58(top), 59(top), 64, 66(bottom), 67(bottom), 72-3,

75(bottom), 78-9, 81(top), 85, 88-9, 95(bottom), 104-5, 101(bottom left), 112(top), 113(top), 122-3, 126-7, 127(top), 210(top), 212-13, 216(top), 249(bottom)
National Motor Museum/Nicky Wright: 66(top), 80-1, 95(top), 99(top), 106, 119(bottom), 126(top), 130(top), 175(top), 176-7
James Taylor, pages: 151(bottom), 156(top), 157(bottom), 171(top), 232(bottom/Rover)